I0438735

Center of Excellence for Geospatial Information Science Research Plan 2013–18

Open-File Report 2013–1189

U.S. Department of the Interior
U.S. Geological Survey

Center of Excellence for Geospatial Information Science Research Plan 2013–18

By E. Lynn Usery

Open-File Report 2013–1189

U.S. Department of the Interior
U.S. Geological Survey

U.S. Department of the Interior
SALLY JEWELL, Secretary

U.S. Geological Survey
Suzette M. Kimball, Acting Director

U.S. Geological Survey, Reston, Virginia: 2013

For more information on the USGS—the Federal source for science about the Earth, its natural and living resources, natural hazards, and the environment, visit http://www.usgs.gov or call 1–888–ASK–USGS.

For an overview of USGS information products, including maps, imagery, and publications, visit http://www.usgs.gov/pubprod

To order this and other USGS information products, visit http://store.usgs.gov

Suggested citation:
Usery, E.L., 2013, Center of Excellence for Geospatial Information Science research plan 2013–18: U.S. Geological Survey Open-File Report 2013–1189, 50 p., http://pub.usgs.gov/of/2013/1189/.

Acknowledgments

Barbara Buttenfield (University of Colorado at Boulder), Cynthia Brewer (Pennsylvania State University), and Keith Clarke (University of California at Santa Barbara) contributed to the development and documentation of this research plan.

Michael Finn, Barbara Poore, Thomas Shoberg, Michael Speak, Larry Stanislawski, and Dalia Varanka of the U.S. Geological Survey contributed to the development and documentation of this research plan.

Contents

Figure

Conversion Factor

SI to Inch/Pound

Multiply	By	To obtain
Length		
meter (m)	3.281	foot (ft)

Center of Excellence for Geospatial Information Science Research Plan 2013–18

By E. Lynn Usery

Abstract

The U.S. Geological Survey Center of Excellence for Geospatial Information Science (CEGIS) was created in 2006 and since that time has provided research primarily in support of *The National Map*. The presentations and publications of the CEGIS researchers document the research accomplishments that include advances in electronic topographic map design, generalization, data integration, map projections, sea level rise modeling, geospatial semantics, ontology, user-centered design, volunteer geographic information, and parallel and grid computing for geospatial data from *The National Map*. A research plan spanning 2013–18 has been developed extending the accomplishments of the CEGIS researchers and documenting new research areas that are anticipated to support *The National Map* of the future. In addition to extending the 2006–12 research areas, the CEGIS research plan for 2013–18 includes new research areas in data models, geospatial semantics, high-performance computing, volunteered geographic information, crowdsourcing, social media, data integration, and multiscale representations to support the Three-Dimensional Elevation Program (3DEP) and *The National Map* of the future of the U.S. Geological Survey.

Introduction and Background

The Center of Excellence for Geospatial Information Science (CEGIS) was established by the Associate Director for Geospatial Information of the U.S. Geological Survey (USGS) in January 2006 as a part of the National Geospatial Program (NGP). CEGIS evolved from a team of cartographic researchers at the Mid-Continent Mapping Center. The team became known as the Cartographic Research group and was supported by the Cooperative Topographic Mapping (CTM), Geographic Analysis and Monitoring (GAM), and Land Remote Sensing (LRS) programs of the Geography Discipline of the USGS from 1999–2005. In 2005, CTM and the Cartographic Research group became a part of the Geospatial Information Office (GIO). In 2006, the Cartographic Research group and its projects (CEGIS, 2013) became the core of CEGIS staff

and research. The Projects for GAM and LRS were completed in 2006 and research in CEGIS became focused on *The National Map*.

With the establishment of CEGIS, the GIO took advantage of an existing contract with the National Research Council (NRC) to develop "A Research Agenda for Geographic Information Science at the U.S. Geological Survey" (*http://books.nap.edu/catalog.php?record_id=12004*). The NRC completed and published the report in 2007. The research agenda in the NRC report became the basis of CEGIS research to support *The National Map* and advance the National Spatial Data Infrastructure (NSDI).

Based on the findings of the 2007 NRC report, several ongoing CEGIS research projects were identified as short-term (2 to 4 years) high priority; these include Automated Data Integration, Generalization, and Developing an Ontology for *The National Map*. The NRC also recommended other high priority short-term projects including User-Centered Design of Web Map Services and Design of an Electronic Topographic Map. Long-term (4 to 8 years) projects recommended by the NRC centered on developing ontology-driven, spatiotemporal, quality-aware, and transaction processing data models. From the existing projects and the recommendations, CEGIS staff developed a research plan including specific projects and resources for the period 2008–15. With the accomplishments of CEGIS and other research toward the goals of the research plan and the changes in the geospatial sciences including new program goals in the NGP, such as the Three-Dimensional Elevation Program (3DEP), and changes in broader science and technology, the CEGIS research plan requires updating. The following discussion provides status and evolution of CEGIS research from 2006 to 2012 and a basic research plan for the period 2013–18. Details of the basic CEGIS accomplishments in the form of presentations and publications are provided in the appendix. In this appendix, the items are organized by CEGIS principal investigators. There is some repetition since CEGIS researchers collaborate on many projects as well as publications and presentations.

Research Projects 2006–12— Accomplishments and Evolution

The NGP provided funding support for CEGIS to conduct the research outlined by the NRC report and the internal research plan developed in CEGIS. All of the proposed and working research projects of CEGIS are inter-related and support the overall goals of the research and *The National Map*. To capture the inter-relations and document the CEGIS research approach, a graphic of the plan in figure 1 was developed and has served as the guiding framework for the activities.

The results and accomplishments of the projects shown in figure 1 from 2006 to 2012 and their evolution to the current (2013) set of projects and activities of CEGIS are discussed below on a project by project basis. The discussion of each project is limited to the basic approach, results, and evolution to current and future projects. The accomplishments of the projects have been presented at mainstream conferences and other forums, published in the literature of cartography and geospatial information science, and in cases implemented within the NGP. Rather than try to include those here, the reader is referred to the publications and presentations listed in the appendix for the many accomplishments and details of the CEGIS work.

Note that the original research agenda prepared by the NRC, as well as the conversion of that agenda to a research plan within the NGP, documented that, to accomplish the research, CEGIS would need 10 Federal research scientists and 10 academic affiliates within the first 5 years of operation. With only six Federal scientists and three academic affiliates, CEGIS has accomplished most of the recommended short-term research and moved some of the work to the operations of the National Geospatial Technical Operations Center (NGTOC). These accomplishments were possible because of a dedicated research staff and the ongoing financial and management support of the NGP.

Design of the Electronic Topographic Map

The USGS has a goal of providing easy public access to geospatial information. One of the best approaches to take in attaining this goal is with topographic maps. Although the NGP began a program to produce topographic maps that

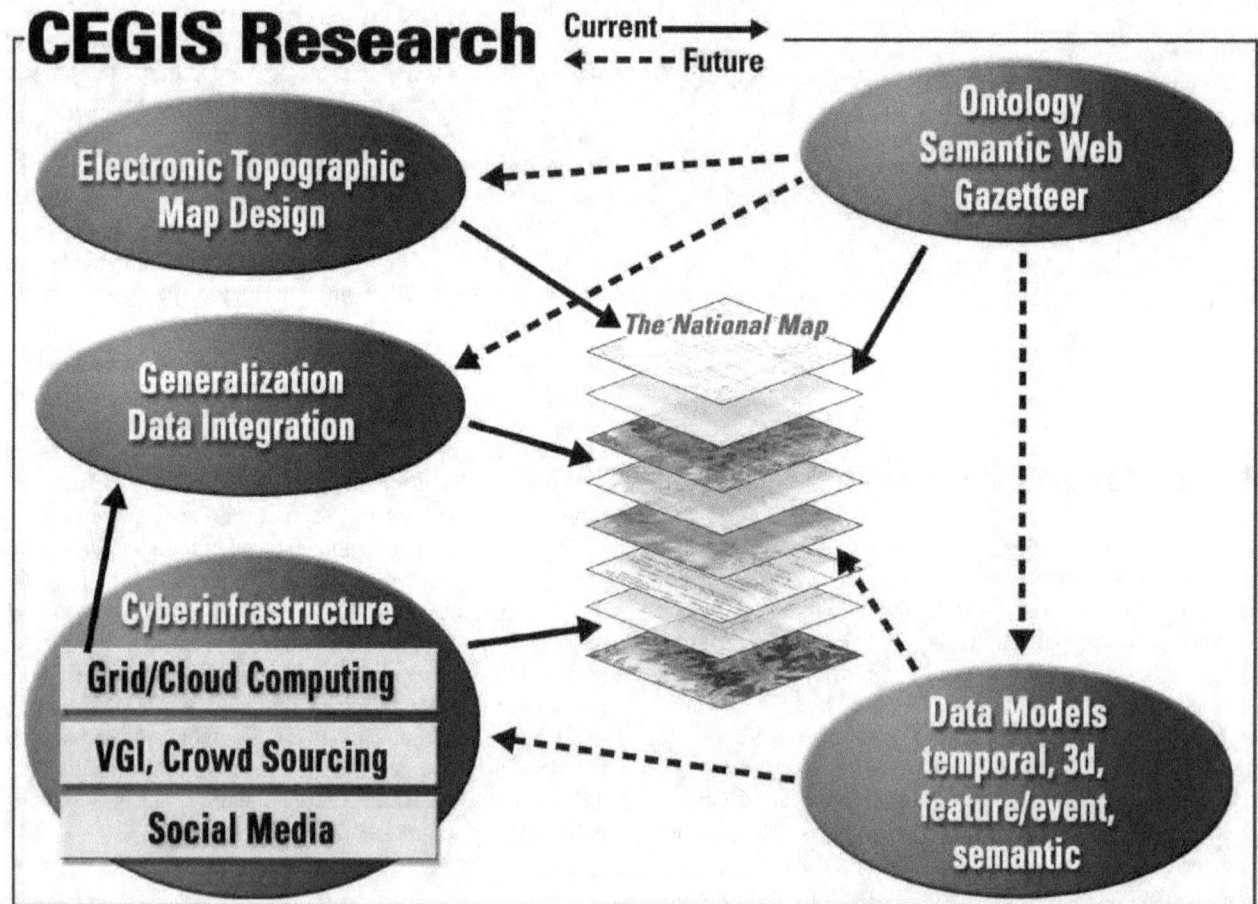

Figure 1.   Center of Excellence for Geospatial Information Science (CEGIS) research projects in progress and planned, 2006–12.

became US Topo from the databases of *The National Map* in 2008, the design of those maps was reliant on symbology and protocols that existed from the previous generation of maps and development of those maps from digital data sources. Much of the design rested on the available symbol tables that the USGS had developed for the standard 1:24,000-scale products. These designs were not optimized for use across multiple scales and multiple output devices including print media and softcopy displays. As a result, and based on the recommendations of the NRC, CEGIS began research to redesign topographic maps for use at multiple scales and in multiple display environments. This research was conducted primarily through grants to the Pennsylvania State University for a new design for electronic topographic maps. Professor Cynthia Brewer and her students led the effort and from 2008 to 2012 and produced a series of new designs. This research is documented in a series of publications and presentations listed in the appendix. The basic designs of this work are complete and are being incorporated into the NGTOC production of US Topo.

Generalization

Geospatial data are accessed, displayed, and used at a variety of resolutions and scales in cartographic and database forms by the USGS user community. To support these uses at various scales, CEGIS conducted research in generalization of geospatial data. The primary objective for this project, as recommended by the NRC (2007), is to research and develop automated methods for generalization to support multiple-scale display and delivery of *The National Map* and other USGS geographic data. Work was structured to use existing Commercial-Off-The-Shelf (COTS) software, mainly Esri ArcGIS tools, and expand functionality as needed to form a standard framework to generalize vector data within *The National Map* databases to scales appropriate for the US Topo and *The National Map* viewer. This functionality requires thorough knowledge of data collection procedures and representation standards for existing map data, along with concepts for appropriate feature representation tailored for cartographic and data modeling purposes. The ultimate goal for this research is to provide a system to automatically generalize data from its most detailed version [for instance, 1:2,400 for the National Hydrography Dataset (NHD) in some areas] to the least detailed scale needed for mapping or modeling (1:17,000,000 for *The National Map* viewer), with the generalization process tailored to the need.

Considering all details, automated generalization is a massively complex problem, and decades of research have been devoted to this topic. For instance, generalization operations may follow either a direct (star) or incremental (ladder) approach depending on the source, target scales, and the density of source data (Buttenfield and others, 2011a). Aside from legibility, operations must include constraints to maintain proper integration within and between generalized data themes, such as among stream channels and between

hydrography and terrain. Work on this project systematically has addressed various generalization issues, which includes development of tools and automated procedures:

- Partition line data into density classes,

- Identify target thinning densities that remove density variations caused by data compilation but maintain variations caused by natural conditions of the terrain and climate,

- Enrich data with priority values for thinning and symbolization,

- Tailor generalization operations to reflect local geographic conditions,

- Validate pruning and simplification results by conflation with benchmark data, and

- Assess the effect of simplification on feature geometry and develop scale-based constraints for feature simplification.

More recent topics include development of methods:

- Assess the effect of generalization on vertical integration,

- Recognize object patterns for feature recognition and subsequent generalization, and

- Implement parallel processing for computationally intense procedures.

The initial focus of this work was with vector-formatted data from *The National Map*, primarily hydrography from the NHD and later transportation from the National Transportation Dataset (NTD) (Stanislawski, 2009; Buttenfield and others, 2011b). To support this research, CEGIS provided a grant to the University of Colorado. From 2008 to 2012, Professor Barbara Buttenfield conducted research for CEGIS in coordination with Larry Stanislawski, initially a contract researcher for the USGS and currently (2013) a USGS Federal employee.

This generalization research was conducted in close coordination with the topographic map design research of Professor Cindy Brewer of Pennsylvania State University and has achieved results that have become operational as a part of *The National Map*, particularly the US Topo product (Brewer and others, 2013). Among the many achievements are a set of tools and procedures that support generalization of data from *The National Map*. Most of the goals of this research have been accomplished and final advancements are planned for the last year of the grant to the University of Colorado to further operationalize the results. Presentations and publications that have resulted from this generalization research are listed in the appendix. The impacts of the work have been important not only to USGS, but also to the world community of generalization researchers.

Data Integration

One of the primary obstacles to the effective use of geospatial data is the various forms in which the data exist. With a multitude of resolutions, accuracies, geometries (raster and vector), thematic attribution and semantics, and temporality, combining datasets through overlay or data fusion is problematic. The process of combining data along all of these aspects is referred to as data integration. The NRC identified data integration as a considerable problem for the eight data layers of *The National Map* and for use of these data layers with other datasets of the USGS (see *http://www.usgs.gov/ngpo/urisa/ datasets.html* for access to USGS datasets).

As a result, CEGIS conducted research on several fronts to develop solutions to these data integration problems. Specific CEGIS projects addressed integration of roads and images and integration of data from *The National Map* with other USGS data, particularly gravity and geophysical data from older surveys. In 2010, CEGIS also began research on feature extraction and conflation from light radar (lidar), also known as light detecting and ranging data. Additionally, the NGTOC of the USGS conducted research particularly to integrate terrain data in the form of contours with data from the NHD. Results to date (2013) from each of these CEGIS projects are documented below and in the appendix.

Roads and Images

The integration of transportation data in the form of roads with digital orthographic images was begun before the formation of CEGIS, but the project became a focus of early CEGIS research. The goal was to use the orthographic image as a base and accomplish the following objectives:

- Determine through visual overlay the user tolerances for mismatches between vector transportation features and corresponding features in the orthographic image.

- Using scale and resolution, form a theory of data integration that would allow automatic determination of whether two datalayers, particularly roads and orthographic images, could be integrated.

- Develop an automated process to integrate roads and images by geometric transformation of the roads to fit the image data based on common ground control points that were generated automatically.

The first two objectives were determined by CEGIS researchers using a survey in which cartographers examined printed overlays of roads and images at 1:24,000-scale and noted discrepancies. These discrepancies were measured and it was concluded that a discrepancy of 6.2 m root mean square error (RMSE) is the threshold at which users perceived the data as not being integrated (Usery and others, 2009).

The third objective was accomplished through a small grant to the University of Southern California (USC). Craig Knoblock was the principal investigator and his group at USC already was engaged in work to integrate map and image data, particularly roads and orthographic images. This group developed a process for automatic control point location and transformation of the vector data to match the orthographic image (Chen and others, 2006). The CEGIS staff replicated this process, to which USGS has rights as a part of the grant, and was able to provide an automated integration solution for roads and image data (Usery and others, 2009). Although internally the USGS never adopted this process in operations for *The National Map*, but rather opted to acquire commercial roads data that already aligned with the orthographic images, the USC group provided a commercial solution through the company Geosemble that was adopted by the National Geospatial-Intelligence Agency and others.

The National Map and Other USGS Data

The USGS has a broad science mission spanning ecosystems, minerals and energy, natural hazards, land use and climate change, and water resources, as well as geospatial information science. *The National Map* provides a foundational infrastructure to serve as a base for geospatial information science and other USGS science research; however, to be most useful the many datasets of the different science programs of the USGS must be integrated with *The National Map*. Therefore, CEGIS has a role in supporting that integration as a part of its basic mission. In 2009, CEGIS began a project to examine integration of geophysical data with *The National Map*. One project examined rejuvenating pre-Global Positioning System geophysical surveys with data from *The National Map* and a second project examined gravity data integration (Shoberg and others, 2010).

Lidar Extraction and Conflation

With the burgeoning availability of lidar elevation data, CEGIS began a project to determine methods and potential for feature extraction from these data sources. CEGIS provided a grant to Keith Clarke at the University of California at Santa Barbara to specifically examine extracting the Warntz network from lidar data. Such an extraction could potentially provide a high-resolution drainage network that could be conflated (integrated) with NHD and other layers of *The National Map*. This work is in early stages and is examining and comparing current commercial and open source software to support the extraction and conflation processes.

Ontology for *The National Map*

The design of ontology, the foundational concepts and structural framework of data, or scientifically, a formal specification of a conceptualization (Gruber, 1993), for *The National Map* was recommended as a CEGIS research project by the NRC. As with generalization and data integration, CEGIS researchers had already begun research on an ontology before the recommendation of the NRC. The purpose of the ontology would be to provide richer semantics to support a data model of topographic information. The richness and potential of such ontology is apparent in that it yields feature components and relations in addition to the standard geographic information system (GIS) feature representations of coordinates, topological relations, and attributes. For example, in an ontological schema, a stream feature includes source, mouth, streambed, streambanks, and crossings; a canyon includes its floor, walls, and head. The representation would be such that these parts and other relations would be accessible and useful in queries and automatic inferencing by a machine. The research had to address multiple facets of building an ontology including developing a taxonomy, vocabulary, and topographic-specific predicates. The project also examined converting legacy datasets from GIS formats to the subject, predicate, and object triples used in the Resource Description Framework (RDF) data model of the Semantic Web and suitable for automatic inferencing and integration with other datasets in the Open Linked Data community.

The research conducted by CEGIS has developed a high level topographic ontology for *The National Map* (Varanka, 2009; 2013). This ontology includes a taxonomy of features, a machine readable vocabulary of these features and their attributes and relations, and data for the vector thematic layers of *The National Map* for specific research test sites converted to RDF to provide instances of the features. A research tool has been developed to convert any geographic area of NHD data from *The National Map* databases to RDF with a supporting data-model specific NHD ontology. Raster features from DEMs have been developed as Ontology Design Patterns for specific named geomorphic features, such as Meteor Crater. The CEGIS converted research data are now in use by others through access to a semantic SPARQL Protocol and RDF Query Language (SPARQL) endpoint on a CEGIS computer server. The CEGIS research effort in this area is recognized internationally and is poised for future work to make the vision of a machine accessible and processable version of *The National Map* a reality. The details of the important accomplishments of CEGIS in developing ontology and semantics for *The National Map* are provided in the publications and presentations listed in the appendix.

User-Centered Design

The CEGIS research agenda recommended by the NRC included a study of User-Centered Design. Although design of an electronic topographic map is a part of information access and dissemination of *The National Map*, a second component is focused on the user and the access provided. CEGIS participated in a user study of *The National Map*. This study included face-to-face and online surveys and provided information on the users and their expectations. The project evolved to include examination of volunteered geographic information, social media and crowdsourcing.

Volunteered Geographic Information

Volunteered geographic information (VGI)—the ability of citizens to use Internet tools to create maps of the world—has become an important area of research in Geographic Information Science (GIScience) in recent years. This new study area was not anticipated in the NRC report. Although the USGS had been using volunteers to help with names and other features on the paper topographic maps, *The National Map* Corps was formed in 2001 to help provide data in digital form. *The National Map* Corps was suspended in 2004, but in the period 2005–10, tools to support VGI became publicly available on the Web. Volunteer mapping projects such as Open Street Map demonstrated the viability of the volunteer approach, and CEGIS, in cooperation with the National Geospatial Technology Operations Center (NGTOC), initiated research to determine how best to incorporate VGI into *The National Map*. The initial pilot projects have been successful and the NGTOC is using volunteers to provide structures data for the State of Colorado in 2013. CEGIS research on VGI has become internationally known, and has demonstrated new methods for evaluating the accuracy of VGI data.

Social Media and Crowdsourcing

Simultaneous with the advent of VGI, the broader area of user input known as crowdsourcing arose. A primary application area of crowdsourcing for geospatial data is in the aftermath of a natural disaster, such as a hurricane or earthquake. USGS scientists already are using crowdsourcing applications such as Did You Feel It to monitor the aftermath of earthquakes. Data mining of crowdsourced data are becoming increasingly important in the arena of "big data" and Cyber-GIS. Analysis of common terms used by citizens to identify map features also will become increasingly important in contributing "bottom up" ontologies to *The National Map* and to other formalized vocabularies being created by data communities across the spectrum of USGS science. This analysis in turn, will contribute to an increasing ability to integrate data from different mission areas of the USGS. CEGIS moved to explore this area of potential for *The National Map* and other areas of USGS science. Details of CEGIS accomplishments in User-Centered Design, VGI, and crowdsourcing are provided in the publications and presentations listed in the appendix.

Multi-Resolution Raster Data

Global modeling applications often require reprojection and resampling of raster datasets. Cartographic research before CEGIS had demonstrated important problems with commercial GIS software when used with global raster data (Usery and others, 2003). Problems included repetition of land areas at the edges of the projection called wrap-around; loss, gain, or both of categorical pixel values; and the inability to resample counts data, such as population numbers. The researchers in the Cartographic Research group that evolved to become CEGIS had developed solutions to these problems using a USGS-developed software package for map projection transformations called mapIMG. This project evolved to a CEGIS project to apply this research and results to *The National Map*. Although *The National Map* does not use global datasets, it does require the projection, transformation, and resampling of huge volumes of raster data for images, terrain, and land cover. Thus, CEGIS evolved the global projections work to address rapid projection and transformation of data from *The National Map* through parallel computing approaches and access to grid-computing technology.

Projections and Parallel/Grid Computing

CEGIS researchers developed a parallel version of the mapIMG program and a user interface to support novice users. Additional developments provided a decision support system for map projection selection and a tutorial that could be accessed online and provide guidance for GIS users. CEGIS researchers collaborated with a team of scientists, led by Sha-owen Wang at the University of Illinois at Urbana-Champaign, on a National Science Foundation grant to develop CyberGIS, the next generation of GIS technology that relies on parallel computing and data intensive science. This project resulted in the implementation of mapIMG on the National Science Foundation (NSF) Science Grid. The project also developed a bulk loader for data from *The National Map*, which was used to load the entire 10-m National Elevation Dataset for the United States to the Science Grid. These data are now available on this grid for scientists and others to use (CyberGIS, 2013). An examination of optimal tile-caching schemes for raster data for use with *The National Map* was begun and continues to the present (2013). Thus, the multi-resolution raster project led to important research into computational capabilities in support of *The National Map*. Results of this continuing and evolving project are presented in the publications and presentations listed in the appendix.

Sea-Level Rise Application

The use of map projections for global data was investigated in the context of environmental models. One such model examined the combination of global data for elevation, population, and land cover to develop models of sea-level rise and the numbers of people and land cover types that would be affected. Although the focus of this research was on the effects of projection transformation and led to important improvements in projecting global raster data, the application of sea-level rise animations was consumed rapidly and became another aspect of CEGIS work. Specifically, CEGIS developed global models of sea-level rise with data for elevation, land cover, and population with 30 arc-second resolution data. Additionally, at the request of a USGS Regional Executive (Tom Casadeval) and an Associate Director (Linda

Gunderson), similar models were developed for the U.S. coastlines with USGS datasets at 30-m resolution for elevation and land cover, and population data from the U.S. Census Bureau rasterized to 30-m cells. Animations produced from this project are available on the CEGIS website (*http://cegis. usgs.gov/sea_level_rise.html*). The presentation and publication results of this work are documented in the appendix.

Application of CEGIS Results to *The National Map* Operations and Use

Results of CEGIS research ultimately are targeted at implementation within the context of *The National Map* and the broader NGP, Core Science Systems, and USGS missions. As a result of this goal, CEGIS researchers participate with NGTOC researchers and developers to support the transition of research into operational activities. Specific examples of such transitions have included the use of CEGIS developed generalization algorithms in the production of US Topo. The process was used to generalize 1:2,400 scale hydrography data in New Jersey, Vermont, portions of Delaware, Mississippi and New York to 1:24,000 scale for use in US Topo. Other examples include the use of the symbology developed as a part of CEGIS research that is being converted to a USGS standard and the implementation of VGI for collecting structures data. Additional transitions, such as using the ontology and semantics taxonomies and vocabularies for *The National Map* to support standards databases and using the CEGIS results from parallel computing research, such as the optimal tile-cache schemes, are planned.

Planned Research 2013–18

Research is a continual building process from previous accomplishments. For CEGIS, this means that the program of work for 2013–18 is planned to continue some of the research begun in the period 2006 to 2012; however, even those projects that are continuing have evolved in objectives, design, and scope. CEGIS work in geospatial semantics evolved from the earlier ontology project. High performance computing and CyberGIS evolved from the multiresolution raster project, and the VGI and crowdsourcing work evolved from the User-Centered Design project. These projects are continuing but are adapting prior work and will form a core part of the plan for future CEGIS research. Additional research needs have arisen because of accomplishments in prior projects, changes in goals and directions of the National Geospatial Program and *The National Map*, and changes in science and technology in general. The strategic science plan for the Core Science Systems Mission Area of the USGS also provides requirements and directions for future CEGIS research (Bristol and others, 2013). These changes dictate the need for a revision of the original CEGIS research plan. In the following "Overview of the 2013–18 Research Plan" section, an overarching research plan is described followed by individual research projects.

Overview of the 2013–18 Research Plan

Rapid developments in geographic information science are driving important changes in the USGS approach to mapping and the provision of geospatial data to support USGS science, Department of Interior management and regulation, and the public's needs. The appearance of commercial geospatial portals and platforms has affected the USGS mission with respect to geospatial data and mapping. The ever-increasing changes in technology also are driving important changes in the USGS and its approach to, and possibilities for, providing geospatial data and mapping. Computational advances, data and information delivery capabilities, and ever-growing uses of geospatial data and maps fundamentally are affecting the USGS. Sensor technology, and its pervasive acceptance and use as a part of everyone's daily life, has important impacts on the geospatial industry in general and USGS in particular. The advent and increasing availability of high-resolution imagery and lidar data are driving the USGS to provide these data to its user community. The capabilities of information technology and delivery through Internet sources and personal devices are changing the ways in which people use geospatial data and the ways in which those data are created. In this richly diverse milieu of data, information, and opportunity, the USGS and CEGIS must focus research resources on problems that are specific and tractable to support geospatial data creation, archiving, and delivery. The CEGIS research plan for 2013 to 2018 defines specific research projects to accomplish a vision of geospatial information creation, archive, access, and delivery. These specific projects and the long-term vision align with the Core Science Systems strategic science plan and the Modular Science Framework (Bristol and others, 2013).

It is anticipated in 2018, users of *The National Map* will be able to access USGS data archives through hand-held devices that have the ability to project large format displays of geospatial and map information, as well as through currently familiar geospatial portals on larger computer systems with large display screens. These data archives will be improved land surface data of higher resolution and accuracies than currently (2013) available and will be three-dimensional and multitemporal, as documented in Bristol and others (2013). Applications for the data will be multifarious and will be user determined. Science users will be routinely using a data-driven science paradigm requiring access to huge (multiterabyte to petabyte) datastores of real and synthetic geospatial data to support data mining, knowledge discovery, modeling, and hypothesis generation and validation. Natural resource and land management organizations, such as many of the Department of Interior Bureaus, will be using Decision Support Systems (DSS) that require and consume data from *The National Map* as a part of the basis of decision making. Requirements will be for multidimensional, spatiotemporal data from semantic database archives and real-time sensor networks, including humans as sensors with hand-held devices.

In such an environment, the USGS must be able to support high-resolution three- and four-dimensional data creation, access, and delivery. During 2013 to 2018, the primary USGS data acquisition efforts will be from the 3DEP. Although the capability exists now (2013) to collect these high-resolution data, the ability to access, query, integrate, and use these data in real-time environments does not yet exist. The geometry of the data is well understood and can be modeled, although currently (2013) all implemented models use a two-dimensional map view, and understanding the semantics and use of those data requires important research.

Thus, CEGIS will work to extend its geospatial semantics research to encompass three-dimensional geometry models, characteristics, and temporal concepts to handle real-time data as well as archived historical data. To handle the tremendous volumes of such data, high performance computing and CyberGIS will become fundamental tools and CEGIS will research these areas to provide solutions. A recent trend for geospatial data has been user participation in creating those data and providing updates and corrections to existing data. Volunteered Geographic Information and crowdsourcing of data and information are expanding at phenomenal rates and the USGS must learn to use these movements to augment traditional sources of data acquisition, correction, and update. Thus, CEGIS will continue research in VGI and crowdsourcing with the aim of providing solutions for *The National Map*.

There is a growing need to integrate the geospatial data of the USGS with other data used in science and applications. This need becomes greater as the USGS begins providing three- and four-dimensional data from the 3DEP program. A priority research area for CEGIS will continue to be this type of data integration. Further, this data integration must be done in a general sense to make data compatible, and in a specific sense to support targeted applications within and external to the USGS.

Finally, CEGIS will engage in a variety of application research projects to help demonstrate the utility of the 3DEP data and information. CEGIS applications research projects will include pilots and test beds in areas such as the generation of derivative products from lidar that are National in scope, examination of resolution impacts on science models, and creation of decision support systems with 3DEP and geospatial semantics. In effect, much of CEGIS research will assist in the development and use of the Modular Science Framework described in Bristol and others (2013).

Spatiotemporal Data Models for 3DEP

As the USGS acquires true three-dimensional data (that is, geographic features with x, y, and z coordinates for each point comprising the feature), there is a need to develop data models that can handle the three-dimensional coordinates. As the frequency of the acquisition of these data improves, a need arises to handle the temporality of the data on a feature-by-feature basis. Thus, features will possess x, y, and z coordinates and a time stamp of the feature date, or perhaps the coordinates will be four dimensional with x, y, z, and t, for each coordinate location. These types of data models have been termed SpatioTemporal Data Models in geospatial research (Peuquet and Duan, 1995; Le and Usery, 2009). Because all current (2013) data models used with *The National Map* are two-dimensional (that is, x and y coordinates with an attribute attached), the development of three-dimensional models is of paramount importance. Although the USGS has been collecting elevation data for more than 40 years, those data all use two-dimensional map models and attach an elevation value as an attribute to x and y coordinates or coordinate locations in a raster matrix. The 3DEP program can be implemented with current two-dimensional models but to realize the complete benefits of the data, a three-dimensional model is needed and will be researched.

Objective

The research will determine an appropriate spatiotemporal model to support 3DEP. The goal of this research is to provide a recommendation for implementation of a data model that handles spatiotemporal data, but also can be implemented in the operational environment of NGP.

Approach

The approach is focused on examining existing spatiotemporal model research and current (2013) implementations in the commercial sector. The research also must include processes to access archive and legacy geospatial data and the following specific steps provide the planned approach to achieve the objectives:

- Survey spatiotemporal models and determine appropriateness for NGP needs,

- Integrate existing research with a spatiotemporal model,

- Provide access to legacy data from a spatiotemporal model,

- Integrate geospatial semantics in a spatiotemporal model, and

- Integrate other USGS data with a spatiotemporal model.

To begin the spatiotemporal data model research, CEGIS will survey the existing research in this area. In the academic environment this has been an active area of research for the last 20 years or more. Many spatiotemporal models have been developed and some are marketed commercially for GIS solutions (Intergraph, 2013), however, none of these models include the recent developments in geospatial semantics,

VGI and crowdsourcing, and high performance computing. These activities already are contributing structures data to *The National Map* and will contribute other data to 3DEP and *The National Map* in the future. Although CEGIS will tap existing research, much remains unexplored to make a viable model to support 3DEP. First and foremost, a model that handles true three-dimensional coordinates on a feature-by-feature basis is required. That model must also support rapid conversion to the triple model of subject, predicate, and object of geospatial semantics and the Semantic Web. Currently (2013), there has been no development of conversion of x,y,z feature geometry that uses the triple model. Maintenance of spatial topology in three-dimensions is another challenge. A simple query of spatiotemporal data, for example, "Find all evacuation routes for a large urban area that account for slope traversal and underpass height limitations and allow movement of people and goods with the capacity for the volume of passengers and freight that must be moved within the time constraints of the evacuation process," indicates the deficiencies of current data models.

Simultaneous to addressing the fundamental problems of three-dimensional and temporal data, the data model research must work with other CEGIS research areas to develop a holistic solution. The developed spatiotemporal model must support geospatial semantics, high performance computing, multiscale data research, VGI and crowdsourcing, and integration with other USGS datasets and data from the public at large. Research in CEGIS must not only determine the three-dimensional data models, but also define protocols for how those models encompass current data in a transition process to those models. The models must also work with other CEGIS research, particularly geospatial semantics, to support the access and use of the 3DEP data in user applications.

Geospatial Semantics

Research concerning geospatial semantics is focused on providing automated access to features, attributes, and relationships in legacy data in a form compatible with automated machine processing. The research must also address the multidimensional characteristics of 3DEP data. Ontologies for geospatial data form a critical aspect of structuring geospatial semantics and the following objectives and approach provide the basis of the research.

Objective

The objective of the research is to provide semantic access to legacy geospatial data and 3DEP to support integration with other USGS science data and modeling. Geospatial data must be structured to allow automated processing of all geospatial data characteristics.

Approach

The approach to the research in geospatial semantics for legacy and 3DEP data requires theoretical and practical steps. The following steps in the approach is designed to extend prior work and address new requirements for geospatial semantics and ontology development:

- Develop semantic interfaces (small data specific ontologies) for legacy data,

- Build topographic predicates for geospatial semantics as reasoning rule extensions,

- Develop example demonstrating value of semantics,

- Extract knowledge from data and data conversion with ontology engineering,

- Collaborate science semantic technology development among ontologists and earth scientists (CEGIS scientists working with other USGS scientists), and

- Research geospatial semantics for 3DEP data.

Future research in semantics must expand the work accomplished in 2006–12, and provide a basis for integration of other USGS datasets with the spatiotemporal data resulting from 3DEP. There currently (2013) are no data models, structures, protocols, or query mechanisms for spatiotemporal data for semantic access and inferencing. The interface of semantically enhanced spatiotemporal data with legacy datasets and other Open Linked data must be researched and developed. A potential benefit of interfacing with legacy datasets is the automated provision of existing or historic information. Operational capability of semantics with legacy data currently (2013) is available and the extension to spatiotemporal data will be a part of the research.

Pattern recognition methods can be applied to legacy datasets to mine features and attributes for items that are embedded in the data but are not resolved explicitly. An example of this is present in NHDFlowlines, whose coastline features intermix natural coastlines with human-made docks and piers. There currently (2013) is no Feature Code (FCODE) for docks and piers in the NHDFlowline schema, but these features may be mined using pattern recognition of regularized shape and size. For example, automatic determination of human-made portions of the coastline can support semantic queries about the portions of a coastline that need special protection during flood events.

As the NGTOC moves forward with the development of a standards database for *The National Map* and the products generated from it, such as US Topo, there is opportunity to leverage the ontology and geospatial semantics research already completed by CEGIS. The taxonomy, vocabulary, and definitions of attributes and relations in the forms of predicates provide a ready base for the development of the standards. Use of this ontology with the standards database also will provide the basis for semantics developments for 3DEP. Research to ensure that the standards developed for the current (2013) geospatial data and for the future 3DEP data are compatible can rely on the already available geospatial ontology developed by CEGIS for *The National Map* (Varanka, 2009; Varanka, 2013).

Specialized types of semantic enhancement will be required for various datasets. Previous research (Varanka and Caro, 2013) identified five different classes of predicates associated with topographic data: (1) part relations within complex features, (2) active verbs providing descriptive relations, (3) active verbs providing process relations, (4) verbs of human intention, and (5) spatial prepositions for forming verb/preposition pairs. These predicates must be implemented as triples of the RDF model, established with topographic instance data, and explored with spatiotemporal data from 3DEP. Inferencing with existing ontologies, such as GeoSPARQL, converted legacy data of *The National Map*, all predicates defined for topographic features, and the plethora of other USGS data must be developed and implemented.

To capture the diversity of data, tools, functions, communities, and applications, the focus of semantics will shift, in the next 5 years, away from the development of singular infrastructure elements, such as standalone ontologies, databases, and models, to ways of connecting and mediating between users and technologies. To achieve the goals of integration with science and VGI communities, and key technologies such as numerical/statistical modeling and social media for targeted applications such as lidar, 3DEP, and DSS, several key stages of work will be required. No singular authoritative body of work will suffice, but local and application-centric ontologies to suit the needs of specific data sets and repositories will be developed and linked using ontology matching.

Reasoning services need to be developed to support service matching or translate between ontologies. For example, the existing NHD ontology will serve as an application ontology with a reasoner service to other required ontologies, such as environmental (water) gaging and quality monitoring data. Metaontologies, for spatial requirements such as spatial dimensions, measurements, map projections, and metadata, will require envelopes and layers to mediate between the Open Geospatial Consortium (OGC) GeoWeb [for example, Web Feature Services (WFS)], with no change of existing spatial data infrastructure resources. Outcomes will be expressed as visualization tools and use cases.

The availability of data from 3DEP requires CEGIS to research the ability of geospatial semantics and ontology to be used with these data. Currently (2013) only x and y (latitude and longitude) coordinates are supported in RDF and semantic geospatial ontologies, such as GeoSPARQL. CEGIS research will expand these capabilities to support x, y, and z coordinates as well as time stamped (t coordinate) features.

High Performance Computing and CyberGIS

High Performance Computing (HPC) is a generic term for research that addresses the use of parallel and super-computing methods to data processing. For geospatial data HPC provides the ability to handle the large (multi gigabyte and terabyte) data volumes and the extensive computations for coordinate transformation and processing. CyberGIS is the term applied to processing geographic data on HPC platforms to implement GIS operations.

Objective

The principal objective is to explore HPC and CyberGIS to support lidar and 3DEP processing. A second objective is to investigate big data approaches with lidar and 3DEP and integration with other USGS science data.

Approach

The approach to HPC and CyberGIS for 3DEP and lidar data must include examination of existing operations with geospatial data and develop new processes in the HPC environment. The following steps were developed to implement the research approach:

- Adapt NGTOC operations to HPC and CyberGIS,

- Determine use of HPC for lidar and 3DEP processing,

- Develop Big Data approaches for lidar and 3DEP,

- Integrate data from *The National Map*, lidar, 3DEP, and other USGS science data using HPC and CyberGIS, and

- Advance CyberGIS to supplement or replace conventional desktop GIS.

Many in the science community are heralding the fourth paradigm of science as data-driven science or data-intensive scientific discovery (Hey and others, 2009). In this science approach, massive datasets are processed to detect anomalies or patterns, develop hypotheses, or address specific problems. The collection of high-resolution elevation data from 3DEP and the availability of high-resolution image and other data will allow 3DEP to drive some of these science investigations; however, use of data-driven science and 3DEP requires computing capability to handle the massive data volumes and the computational needs. Researchers in CEGIS in high performance computing have begun a process of investigating the possibilities of this science approach. Future research will refine and establish computational capability and CyberGIS as the next generation of GIS that can solve problems using the massive datasets available through parallel processing and sophisticated computational algorithms. Therefore, CEGIS research must address this computational and data handling problem. The start with map projections and tile caching are the beginnings of determining capabilities of CyberGIS to support 3DEP and future USGS needs in data-driven science.

CEGIS researchers will work closely with NGTOC developers to identify areas of NGTOC operations to which

HPC can effectively be applied. One example described during 2006–12 research synopsis, cartographic and data model generalization of *The National Map* data themes, involves computationally intensive processes for data enrichment and generalization operations with vertically integrated results. Future CEGIS research is anticipated to develop parallel processing approaches to implement these processes at the National level for efficient sequential updates of generalized databases. This development for *The National Map* data is expected to enhance the content and integration of data themes distributed through *The National Map* and The National Atlas of the United States.

VGI, Crowdsourcing, and Social Media

The evolution of the User-Centered Design research has been affected by developments in VGI, crowdsourcing and social media. The CEGIS research agenda has evolved to integrate these developments in the next generation of geospatial data along with the 3DEP data collection and operations.

Objective

The research objective is to integrate VGI, social media, and citizen science with USGS science and data programs. This objective is multifaceted and continues to evolve because of the rapid advancement of these technologies.

Approach

Examination of methods to integrate these technologies form a core component of the research approach. The following items have been identified as critical steps in the research approach:

- Integrate VGI and crowdsourcing with NGP data and operations,

- Develop access and use of social media for NGP data and operations,

- Investigate interdisciplinary science and data integration using VGI, crowdsourcing, and social media,

- Investigate Big Data from VGI, crowdsourcing, and social media, and

- Investigate the use of *The National Map* on hand-held devices.

Volunteered Geographic Information and crowdsourcing are changing the methods in which geospatial data are collected and used. The USGS projects in VGI have demonstrated that this is a viable source for data collection for *The National Map*. Beyond that, these movements and technologies will change the entire approach and concept of mapping, including topographic mapping. Therefore, CEGIS research will need to examine and participate in these movements as a part of its basic research agenda.

The impacts of VGI and crowdsourcing in mitigation and response to multihazard disasters are just beginning to be explored. These technologies and social media will be explored in CEGIS research as they develop and become more of a part of the mainstream data in geospatial and other operations.

Scientific practices in the earth and environmental sciences are changing rapidly because of a number of factors:

- Scientists are now called on to address problems that demand interdisciplinary collaboration. The recent realignment of USGS into issue-driven mission areas reflects this new approach to problem solving.

- Sensors of many different types are generating vast amounts of data that are available to researchers through computing infrastructures. Scientists are mining data feeds from social media such as Flickr, Twitter, and Facebook to analyze responses to natural disasters and to uncover public reactions to the natural world. Data-driven science has been called a "fourth paradigm" that will enhance the existing paradigms of experimental, theoretical and computational science (Hey and others, 2009).

- Nonscientists are using new computing infrastructures and mobile applications to "mash-up" disparate datasets on the Internet. Citizen scientists are using these same technologies to collect observational data for scientific projects, and in many cases, to inform the designs and trajectories of these projects. At the recent Citizen Science Workshop, sponsored by the Community for Data Integration, scientists from across the USGS and other organizations presented examples of citizen science projects with which they were involved. Topics included climate change, phenology, invasive species, animal diseases, mobile-phone detection and analysis of cricket chirps, volcanic ash flow, rapid earthquake detection, and VGI for *The National Map* (USGS, 2012).

- The availability of data from *The National Map* and 3DEP on mobile devices provides additional uses in USGS science applications.

The National Map in the Tactical Plan has been described as the "most fundamental aspect of [the USGS] Data Integration direction is *The National Map*, which will provide the trusted, base geospatial information for science investigations." (Carswell, 2008, p. 47). *The National Map* is supposed to "accelerate science investigations," resulting from the 2007 USGS science strategy (U.S. Geological Survey, 2007). For *The National Map* to fully assume this function, new trends and future directions of information technology and scientific practice must be understood and translated into our application domains. The CEGIS research program will be extended to investigate new information and communication technologies that are affecting methods by which scientists collaborate, synthesize new research from massive datasets, and communicate results of these new discoveries to decision makers and the public.

Interdisciplinary Science and Data Integration

Interdisciplinary science and data integration are difficult processes. These activities suffer from misalignments that result from different ways of working, terminologies, and data structures. Research into the implications of the Semantic Web—a machine-readable markup structure for data that will allow computers to understand and act on the semantic relationships embedded in data objects—has been a prominent focus of CEGIS work in the ontology project. Recognizing that top-down single discipline ontologies are not sufficient to fully capture the semantic differences between scientific communities, during the next 5 years the ontology project will move in the direction of mediating between disparate users and technologies. A key to this effort is understanding how local perceptions, as captured by VGI and social media, can inform the design of semantic technologies.

Big Data

Providing access to the massive volumes of data that fuel interdisciplinary, data-driven science at the USGS is being addressed in part by the CyberGIS project supported by CEGIS. This project focuses on building the tubes through which data will travel as well as the tools for analysis; however, important questions remain. For example, in the data deluge, who decides which data are important? One part of the answer lies in data mining. Many of the tools and techniques of data mining, natural language processing, and image analysis are being developed by social media researchers. For example, in the aftermath of Hurricane Sandy, Civil Air Patrol photographs are being used by volunteers to evaluate damage—a task that cannot yet be executed with computers (Munro and others, 2013).

Another part of the answer lies in promoting better data curation. Data curation—managing data to ensure they are fit for contemporary use and available for discovery and reuse—goes beyond traditional data management into issues of authentication, archiving, preservation, retrieval, and representation. For example, data curators are making use of geospatial narrative to analyze and predict events through space and time. Many of these innovative approaches to data curation have been pioneered by social media researchers (Liu, 2012).

Citizen Science

Citizen science, also called public participation in science or participatory sensing, is a natural two-way bridge between the USGS and the American public. As described above, it is already being used by a number of USGS disciplines including the NGP. Not only can citizens collect data that are important to understand changes that are taking place in the environment, but citizens can collaborate in the collective design and investigation of real world problems. Aspects of citizen science in which CEGIS researchers are involved include:

- Use of remotely sensed images for integration of participant and social data,

- Extracting value from massive volumes of data,

- Design of technologies for mobile, collaborative, and distributed interaction,

- Determining infrastructures for sensor integration,

- Providing simple visualization methods for presenting data to various groups of users,

- Determining system architectures that promote security and privacy for citizen science, and

- Establishing guidelines on the policies and practices of data collection for citizen science.

Integrating Other USGS Data

A key research requirement for any new data development, such as 3DEP, is integration with existing data and processes. This element of the CEGIS research plan is dependent on examining USGS data acquired for specific research applications in the USGS science mission. The research will examine methods of integration of these dispirate datasets.

Objective

The overall objective is to integrate data from *The National Map* with selected USGS science datasets to support visualization, analysis, modeling, and decision making efforts of the USGS, other government agencies, and the general public. The integration process must support the specific applications of the science data.

Approach

To address integration of 3DEP and other data from *The National Map* with USGS science data a series of specific projects and datasets will be examined. The following steps provide a synopsis of the approach:

- Assess the resiliency and scalability of multihazards supply chain networks with the use of integrated geospatial data,

- Integrate geology with geospatial data from 3DEP and *The National Map,*

- Integrate 3DEP and *The National Map* with near-surface geology and faults for earthquake and landslide risk maps, and

- Integrate geophysical and geologic data, 3DEP and *The National Map* for applications in economics, health, safety, and energy.

Geospatial data are critical to disaster mitigation and recovery. The USGS and the NGP in particular have a role in supplying geospatial data in the form of maps and images from a variety of sources including *The National Map*. To be effective in disaster recovery, these data need to be integrated with other data sources. Thus, CEGIS has begun assessment of the resiliency and scalability of multihazards supply chain networks with the use of integrated geospatial data. This project requires integrating data from *The National Map* with other datasets in the supply chain. Research questions surround resiliency of the network and times to recovery after a substantial disaster such as an earthquake or hurricane.

A primary tool in the inventory and exploitation of fossil fuels and mineral resources throughout the Nation is knowledge of local geology. An instrument that could greatly enhance this effort would be a 3DEP integration of geology with geospatial data from *The National Map*. This integration would involve a four-fold approach: completion of the integration of the surface geologic maps for the Nation; catalog and assembly of pre-existing three-dimensional (3-D) geology data from local regions; interpolation and integration of the local 3-D geology data where they exist with inferences of surface geology maps where no models currently are available; and, quality control of complete models using borehole data as well as existing geophysical data. CEGIS researchers are collaborating with USGS geologists on this work.

Another part of this research includes a categorization of geologic hazards for the Nation. Emphases on earthquake potential and landslide risk largely are based on surface faults and hill slopes; however, subsurface fault locations are important not only in earthquake prone areas but in stable regions as well because these subsurface faults can experience reactivation during extensive injection well pumping as has been experienced in Colorado and Texas (Hsieh and Bredehoft, 1981; Frolich and others, 2011). Near-surface geology also is a key component in landslide initiation, particularly with respect to construction overburden removal. Again, there are areas where these considerations have been considered and mapped. The challenge is to integrate these data with geospatial data from *The National Map*, which results in a uniform, comprehensive database.

There is still a great need to amass and integrate important geophysical and geologic databases with the geospatial data. Many of these databases that do exist have little or no metadata associated with each entry, making their quality and reliability suspect. The success of integrating one such database (gravity) implies that the task is not intractable (Shoberg and Stoddard, 2013). The ability to access and utilize large quantities of geophysical and geologic data with some estimates on accuracy and reliability would form a substantial backdrop for many applications in economics, health, safety, and energy.

CEGIS will continue to participate in the USGS Community for Data Integration in a variety of projects. Many of these will be application specific, but the CEGIS role will continue to be integration of data from *The National Map* and integration of CEGIS research and results in the community.

Multiscale Representation

Although the data of 3DEP and *The National Map* are collected and archived with specific resolution and accuracy, the applications of the data require representation at many different scales and resolutions. Thus, processes that suport allow multiscale representations of the data must be researched, developed, and made available.

Objective

This research will identify relations between map scale and geomorphological characteristics of cartographic features to automate generalization and define ontology patterns for feature extraction. It also will determine effects of high-resolution elevation and hydrographic data on science models.

Approach

The approach to multiscale representation is focused primarily on high-resolution elevation data, resulting from 3DEP, and hydrography. These two data categories are the basic components of topographic representation and two specific steps in the approach have been defined:

- Derive national scale-dependent elevation drainage channels, and

- Assess resolution impacts on science models.

The use of high resolution elevation data for derivation of drainage channels and the ability to use those derived channels in concert with existing hydrographic data will be investigated. Elevation and hydrography are basic inputs to many science and environmental models, and the value or impact of such inputs from 3DEP requires investigation. An assumption that the higher resolution of these spatial data will improve model results may be invalid and must be explored.

Derivation of National Scale-Dependent Elevation-Derived Drainage Channels

Preservation of the quality of our Nation's water resources is a primary concern to current and future generations. A fundamental component to preservation and modeling of surface-water quality is accurate mapping and monitoring of these resources. Through a number of programs, the USGS

uses and maintains thousands of gaging stations to monitor the quality and amount of water flowing through rivers and lakes in the country, and these data subsequently are distributed to the public in near real-time. The USGS StreamStats program integrates gage measurements with terrain data to estimate streamflow statistics for gaged and ungaged rivers in the NHD; however, the surface-water flowline features in the NHD (NHDFlowlines) have been compiled from a variety of sources, scales, collection standards, and climate conditions during the past 30 to 40 years. Consequently, feature representations and densities are not consistent over the United States, which complicates hydrologic modeling and analysis.

Continuing earlier work and in coordination with concurrent elevation-derivative projects, this CEGIS research will integrate the drainage channel derivation process with other related data to enhance the process to form consistently defined stream channels tailored for a specific scale. Related datasets will include, but are not limited to, estimates for slope, soil permeability and depth, subsurface bedrock and drainage conditions, and surface runoff. Subsequently, effects of non-natural drainage diversions—such as dams, canals, and pipes—will be incorporated into the extraction process. The research will address resolution dependencies with scale-specific extraction and landscape type, along with testing the latest approaches for extracting channels in complex drainage situations, and the use of efficient parallel processing methods for sequential updates on a national level. This research will greatly enhance the NHD by providing automated methods to consistently map drainage channels for the Nation in a timely fashion.

Resolution Impacts on Science Models

With the availability of high-resolution, multi-dimensional spatiotemporal data, many models used in USGS science can potentially yield better results; however, this is not always true. In some cases, the higher-resolution data no longer fit the parameters of the original models, which were designed for application with lower resolution geospatial input data. Determining which models benefit from the higher-resolution and multi-dimensional spatiotemporal data is a research question. In a limited manner, CEGIS research will attempt to address this question, again based on user needs.

Research for Applications and Operational Investigations

In addition to the basic research topics presented above, CEGIS will conduct applications research and some operational investigations for National programs of the NGP. The 3DEP program and CEGIS basic research will provide spatiotemporal data with three-dimensional coordinates and time for each coordinate set and geographic feature. The use of these data in USGS science and other applications needs to be researched and developed. Following are some initial targets for applications and operational investigations.

Objective

The research will help develop methods, tools, processes, and systems to support use of lidar and 3DEP in USGS science programs. Determination of derivative products of National significance is a part of this effort. The use of Decision Support Systems (DSS) with 3DEP, *The National Map*, and USGS science data are of critical importance and are a part of the research objectives.

Approach

The approach requires determining products that are National in scope and can be used in DSS. The following specific steps comprise the approach to be used in the CEGIS research:

- Determine the set of National derivative products of lidar point clouds to be supported with 3DEP, and

- Investigate DSS with 3DEP and geospatial semantics.

National Derivative Products of Lidar Point Clouds for 3DEP

The development of derivative products from lidar point cloud data, which will be acquired as a part of 3DEP, is a research area for CEGIS in the next 5 years. Surface-water hydrography as a part of surface network extraction is one such product already under investigation by CEGIS researchers. Standard derivative products of elevation data, such as shaded relief, synthetic stereo images, slope, and aspect, require no investigation, but can be derived on a National basis with conventional GIS algorithms and software; however, the use of the lidar point cloud to supply additional products based on the multiple returns and intensity signals requires investigation. Products indicating vegetation characteristics and urban structure, which are developable from the multiple returns and intensity of lidar, are candidates for derivatives of National importance. CEGIS researchers will need to work with application domain experts and lidar specialists to determine these types of products and the processes for deriving them from lidar.

Decision Support Systems (DSS) with 3DEP and Geospatial Semantics

The availability of semantically enhanced, high-resolution, multidimensional spatiotemporal data offers promise for developing DSS for science, natural resources, and land management. With the provision of multidimensional data and semantic inferencing, the development of DSS will be a natural extension of the data capabilities and management tools. The focus will be a demonstration project that illustrates the value of geospatial semantics in a decision support system. CEGIS will have to connect with the USGS science community, perhaps though the USGS Commuity for Data Inegration and projects with the Powell Center, to best approach this area, but it provides an excellent opportunity to demonstrate the value of 3DEP and semantically enhanced datasets.

Conclusions

In the report concerning a research agenda for GIScience in the USGS (NRC 2007), which became the basis of CEGIS research for the 2008–12 timeframe, the NRC stated that CEGIS should focus on several high priority, high visibility projects that had potential for a return on the research investment to establish credibility and a reputation in GIScience research. Topics identified in this group included generalization, data integration, and electronic topographic map design. CEGIS did invest in these research areas and as a result has generated results that have been publicized, published, and subsequently accepted by the international research community and are being implemented in the operational programs of *The National Map*. As a result of these efforts CEGIS has established an international reputation for conducting relevant high-quality GIScience research.Additional recommendations of the NRC report included longer term projects in which CEGIS has also invested and made important progress. The success of CEGIS researchers in making accomplishments that have been presented and published in the scientific literature is indicated in the appendix. Based on these accomplishments, CEGIS can advance planned research in support of *The National Map* and begin new research in areas that have arisen because of changes in program goals and advances and changes in science and technology. The ability of the CEGIS research core to orchestrate and accomplish the research objectives presented in this strategic plan will depend on available funding and continued collaborations and partnerships with other USGS research groups, federal agencies, and academic affiliates.

New research areas are built around continuing research in geospatial semantics, VGI and crowdsourcing, high performance computing, and data integration and applications of data from *The National Map;* new investigations of multidimensional, spatiotemporal data models; and the potential products, requirements, and applications of lidar and 3DEP. CEGIS reseach is a critical part of the strategic direction and foundation of the Modular Science Framework described in the Core Science Systems strategy by Bristol and others (2013).

References

Brewer, C.A, Stanislawski, L.V., Buttenfield, B.P., Sparks, K.A., McGilloway, J., Howard, M.A., 2013, Automated thinning of road networks and road labels for multiscale design of *The National Map* of the United States: Cartography and Geographic Information.

Bristol, R.S., Euliss, N.H., Jr., Booth, N.L., Burkardt, Nina, Diffendorfer, J.E., Gesch, D.B., McCallum, B.E., Miller, D.M., Morman, S.A., Poore, B.S., Signell, R.P., and Viger, R.J., 2013, U.S. Geological Survey core science systems strategy—Characterizing, synthesizing, and understanding the critical zone through a modular science framework: U.S. Geological Survey Circular 1383–B, 33 p.

Buttenfield, B.P., Stanislawski, L.V., and Brewer, C.A., 2011a, A comparison of star and ladder strategies for intermediate scale processing of USGS National Hydrography Dataset, 14th ICA/ISPRS Workshop on Generalization and Multiple Representations, Paris, France.

Buttenfield, B.P., Stanislawski, L.V., and Brewer, C.A,. 2011b, Adapting generalization tools to physiographic diversity for the United States National Hydrography Dataset, Cartography and Geographic Information Science, v. 38, no. 3, p. 289–301.

Carswell, W.J., Jr., 2008, *The National Map* 2.0 tactical plan—"Toward the (integrated) national map: U.S. Geological Survey Open-File Report 2008–1263, 57 p.

CEGIS, 2013, Current research for *The National Map*, accessed July 10, 2013 at *http://cegis.usgs.gov/projects.html*.

Chen, C.C., Knoblock, C.A., and Shahabi, C., 2006, Automatically conflating road vector data with orthoimagery: Geoinformatica, v. 10, no. 4, p. 495–530.

CyberGIS, 2013, Tools: NED fusion tool, accessed on July 10, 2013, at *http://cgwiki.cigi.uiuc.edu:8080/mediawiki/index.php/Tools:NED_Fusion_Tool*.

Frolich, C., Potter, E., Hayward, C., and Stump, B., 2011, The Dallas-Fort Worth earthquake sequence: October 2008 through May 2009: Seismological Society of America, v. 101, p. 327–340.

Gruber, T., 1993, A translation approach to portable ontology specifications: Knowledge Acquisition, v. 5, n. 2, p. 199–220, accessed August, 19, 2013, at *http://tomgruber.org/writing/ontolingua-kaj-1993.htm*.

Hey, T., Tansley, S., and Tolle, K., 2009, The fourth paradigm: Data intensive scientific discovery: Microsoft Corporation, Redmond, Washington.

Hsieh, P., and Bredehoft, J., 1981, A reservoir analysis of the Denver earthquakes: A case study of induced seismicity: Journal of Geophysical Research, v. 86, p. 903–920.

Intergraph, 2013, Products: ERDAS Apollo, accessed on July 10, 2013, at *http://geospatial.intergraph.com/products/ERDASAPOLLO/Details.aspx*.

Le, Y., and Usery, E.L., 2009, Adding time to GIS, *in* Madden, M., ed., Manual of geographic information systems, American Society for Photogrammetry and Remote Sensing: Bethesda, Maryland, p. 311–332.

Liu, S.B., 2012, Socially distributed curation of the Bhopal disaster: A case of grassroots heritage in the crisis context, *in* Giaccardi, E., ed., Heritage and social media: Understanding and experiencing heritage in a participatory culture: Routledge, Cambridge, UK, p. 30–55.

Munro, R., Schnoebelen, T., Erle, S., 2013, Quality analysis after action report for the crowdsourced aerial imagery assessment following Hurricane Sandy: Proceedings of the 10th International ISCRAM Conference, Baden-Baden Germany, Comes T., Fiedrich, F., Fortier, S., Geldermann, J., and Yang, L., eds., *http://idibon.com/wp-content/uploads/2013/05/ISCRAM2013_Paper.pdf*.

NRC, 2007, A Research agenda for geographic information science at the United States Geological Survey: National Academy of Sciences, National academies press, Washington, D.C., 143 p.

Peuquet, D.J., and Duan, N., 1995, An event-based spatio-temporal data model (ESTDM) for temporal analysis of geographical data: International Journal of Geographical Information Systems, v. 9, no. 1, p. 7–24.

Shoberg, T., and Stoddard, P.R., 2013, Integrating stations from the North America Gravity Database into a local GPS-based land gravity survey: Journal of Applied Physics, v. 89, 76–83.

Shoberg, T., Stoddard, P.R., and Finn, M.P., 2012, Rejuvenating pre-GPS Era geophysical surveys using *The National Map*: Journal of Surveying Engineering, v. 138, no. 2, p. 57–65.

Stanislawski, L.V., 2009, Feature pruning by upstream drainage area to support automated generalization of the United States National Hydrography Dataset: Computers, Environment, and Urban Systems, v. 33, no. 5, p. 325–333.

Usery, E.L., Finn, M.P., Cox, J.D., Beard, T., Ruhl, S., and Bearden, M., 2003, Projecting global datasets to achieve equal areas, cartography and geographic information science, v. 30, no. 1, p. 69–79.

Usery, E.L., Finn, M.P., and Starbuck, M., 2009, Data layer integration for *The National Map* of The United States: Cartographic Perspectives, v. 62, p. 28–41.

Varanka, D., 2009, A topographic feature taxonomy for a U.S. national topographic mapping ontology: International Cartography Conference, Santiago, Chile.

Varanka, D., 2013, Geospatial semantics and ontology, accessed on July 10, 2013, at *http://cegis.usgs.gov/ontology.html*.

Varanka, D., and Caro, H., 2013, Spatial relation predicates for topographic data triples *in* Martin Raubal, Andrew Frank, and David Mark, Eds., Cognitive and linguistic aspects of geographical space: New Perspectives on Geographic Information Research, Lecture Notes in Geoinformation and Cartography, Springer, p. 175–193.

U.S. Geological Survey, 2007, Facing tomorrow's challenges—U.S. Geological Survey science in the decade 2007–2017: U.S. Geological Survey Circular 1309, x + 70 p.

U.S. Geological Survey, 2012, USGS Citizen Science Workshop Agenda, accessed on July 12, 2013, at *https://my.usgs.gov/confluence/display/cdi/USGS+Citizen+Science+Workshop+Agenda*.

Appendix

This appendix provides a listing of publications and presentations that resulted from CEGIS research in the 2006-2012 timeframe. It is included to provide the reader with a single document that includes presentations and publications of all CEGIS Federal and affiliate faculty researchers. The list is organized by topic, then by individual researchers for each topic and contains the following content.

CEGIS Research Publications and Presentations
2006–2012
Publications and Presentations 2007–2012
Electronic Topographic Map Design Research

Dr. Cynthia A. Brewer

November 2012

Products related to CEGIS funding

Peer-Reviewed Publications

Roth, R.E., Brewer, C.A., and Stryker, M.S., 2011, A typology of operators for maintaining legible map designs at multiple scales: Cartographic Perspectives, no. 68, p. 29–64.

Buttenfield, B.P., Stanislawski, L.V., and Brewer, C.A., 2011, Adapting generalization tools to physiographic diversity for the USGS National Hydrography Dataset, *in* U.S. National Report to the International Cartographic Association: Cartography and Geographic Information Science, vol. 38, no. 3, p. 289–301.

Butzler, S.J., Brewer, C.A., and Stroh, W.J., 2011, Establishing classification and hierarchy in populated place labeling for multi-scale mapping for *The National Map*: Cartography and Geographic Information Science, vol. 38, no. 2, p. 100–109.

Brewer, C.A., and Buttenfield, B.P., 2010, Mastering map scale—Balancing workloads using display and geometry change in multi-scale mapping: Geoinformatica, vol.14, no. 2, p. 221–239.

Brewer, C.A., and Buttenfield, B.P., 2007, Framing guidelines for multi-scale map design using databases at multiple resolutions: Cartography and Geographic Information Science, vol. 34, no. 1, p. 3–15.

Refereed Conference Proceedings

Brewer, C.A., Stanislawski, L.V., Buttenfield, B.P., Raposo, P., Sparks, K., and Howard, M., 2012, Multiscale design for *The National Map* of the United States—Road thinning for topographic mapping: Proceedings, AutoCarto International Symposium on Automated Cartography, Columbus, Ohio, September, 2012.

Stanislawski, L.V., Briat, M.O., Punt, E., Howard, M., Brewer, C.A., and B.P. Buttenfield, 2012, Density stratified thinning of road networks to support automated generalization for *The National Map* [abs.]: Proceedings, Workshop of the International Cartographic Association Commission on Generalisation and Multiple Representation, 15th, Istanbul, Turkey, September 2012.

Brewer, C.A., Buttenfield, B.P., and Stanislawski, L.V., 2011, Choosing between geometry change and display change for multi-scale mapping—The role of elimination in design: Proceedings, International Cartographic Conference 2011 (ICC2011), 25th, Paris, France, July 2011, p. 11.

Brewer, C.A., and Raposo, P., 2011, Comparison of topographic map designs for overlay on orthoimage backgrounds: Proceedings, International Cartographic Conference 2011 (ICC2011), 25th, Paris, France, July 2011, 10 p.

Brewer, C.A., Thatcher, J.E., and Butzler, S.J., 2011, Combining varied federal data sources for multiscale map labeling of populated places and airports for *The National Map* of the United States: Proceedings, Workshop of the International Cartographic Conference Commission on Generalisation and Multiple Representation, Paris, France, June/July 2011.

Buttenfield, B.P., Stanislawski, L.V., and Brewer, C.A., 2011, A comparison of star and ladder generalization strategies for intermediate scale processing of USGS National Hydrography Dataset Workshop: Proceedings, Workshop of the International Cartographic Conference Commission Commission on Generalisation and Multiple Representation, Paris, France, June/July 2011.

Brewer, C.A., Hanchett, C.L., Buttenfield, B.P., and Usery, E.L., 2010, Performance of map symbol and label design with format and display resolution options through scale for *The National Map:* Proceedings, AutoCarto 2010, Orlando, Florida, November 2010, p. 6. (CD-ROM).

Stroh, W.J., Butzler, S.J., and Brewer, C.A., 2010, Establishing classification and hierarchy in populated place labeling for multiscale mapping for *The National Map*: Prcoceedings, AutoCarto 2010, Orlando, Florida, November 2012, p. 6. (CD-ROM).

Wilmer, J.M., and Brewer, C.A., 2010, Application of the radical law in generalization of national hydrography data for multiscale mapping: Proceedings, AutoCarto 2010, Orlando, Florida, November 2010, p. 6. (CD-ROM).

Buttenfield, B.P., Stanislawki, L.V., and Brewer, C.A., 2010, Multiscale representations of water—Tailoring generalization sequences to specific physiographic regimes: Proceedings, GIScience 2010, 6th, Zurich, Switzerland, September 2010, p. 6. (selected as a 'top four short paper' at the conference; refereed proceedings distributed on USB.)

Brewer, C.A., Buttenfield, B.P., and Usery, E.L., 2009, Evaluating generalizations of hydrography in differing terrains for *The National Map* of the United States: Proceedings, International Cartographic Conference (ICC2009), 24th, Santiago, Chile, November 2009, p.12.

Brewer, C.A., and Akella, M.K., 2008, Multi-resolution multi-scale topographic map design–Toward a new look for *The National Map*: Proceedings, AutoCarto 2008, Shepherdstown, West Virginia, September 2008, p. 12. (CD-ROM).

Stryker, M., Roth, R.E., and Brewer, C.A., 2008, ScaleMaster.org—Illustrating and constructing the multi-scale mapping process: Proceedings, International Conference on Geographic Information Science, 5th, GIScience 2008, Park City, Utah, September 2008.

Presentatons

Brewer, C.A., Robinson, A.C., and Raposo, P., 2012, Mapping around the world—A cartographic study abroad experience: North American Cartographic Information Society (NACIS) Annual Meeting, Portland Oregon.

Raposo, P., Sparks, K., and Brewer, C.A., 2012, Techniques for cartographic presentation of upsampled raster land cover data: North American Cartographic Information Society (NACIS) Annual Meeting, Portland, Oregon.

Brewer, C.A., Stanislawski, L.V., Buttenfield, B.P., Raposo, P., Sparks, K., and Howard, M., 2012, Multiscale design for *The National Map* of the United States—Road thinning for topographic mapping: AutoCarto 2012, Columbus, Ohio, September 2012.

Stanislawski, L.V., Briat, M.O., Punt, E., Howard, M., Buttenfield, B.P., and Brewer, C.A., 2012, Density stratified thinning of road networks to support automated generalization for *The National Map*: International Cartographic Association (ICA) Commission on Generalisation and Multiple Representation Workshop, Istanbul,Turkey.

Brewer, C.A., invited commentator, 2012: US Topo, video produced by J. Maxwell, U.S. Geological Survey, Department of Interior, gallery.usgs.gov/videos/568 or www.youtube.com/watch?v=hv0jxsW3qgY.

Brewer, C.A., Robinson, A.C., and Raposo, P., 2012, National mapping around the world: Center of Excellence for Geospatial Information Science (CEGIS) Annual Research Meeting, Rolla, Missouri.

Brewer, C.A., Sparks, K.A., and Raposo, P., 2012, Multiscale design for *The National Map,* 2011/12: Center of Excellence for Geospatial Information Science (CEGIS) Annual Research Meeting, Rolla, Missouri.

Sparks, K.A., Raposo, P., and Brewer, C.A., 2012, Multiscale land cover design for *The National Map*: Center of Excellence for Geospatial Information Science (CEGIS) Annual Research Meeting, Rolla, Missouri.

Sparks, K.A., Raposo, P., and Brewer, C.A., 2012, Multiscale land cover design for *The National Map*: Center of Excellence for Geospatial Information Science (CEGIS) Annual Research Meeting, Rolla, Missouri.

Brewer, C.A., and Raposo, P., 2012, Multiscale design for *The National Map* of the U.S.: Association of American Geographers, Middle States Division annual meeting, Shippenburg, Pennsylvania.

Brewer, C.A., 2012, Multiscale design for T*he National Map* of the U.S.: Division Geoinformation, Bundesamt für Kartographie und Geodäsie (BKG; Federal Agency for Cartography and Geodesy), Frankfurt am Main, Germany.

Brewer, C.A., 2012, Multiscale design for *The National Map* of the U.S.: Abu Dhabi Systems and Information Center, Abu Dhabi, United Arab Emirates.

Brewer, C.A., 2012, Multiscale design for *The National Map* of the U.S.: Center for Spatial Information Science, The University of Tokyo—Hongo, Tokyo, Japan.

Brewer, C.A., 2012, Multiscale design for *The National Map* of the U.S.: Invited colloquium, Department of Geography, Ohio State University, Columbus, Ohio.

Brewer, C.A., 2011, Multiscale redesign of *The National Map* with USGS: invited presentation, Coffee Hour, Department of Geography Colloquium, Pennsylvania State University. Broadcast and posted online through the department's Coffee Hour to Go program: e-education.mediasite.commediasite/Viewer/?peid= 982eb32231c84250b725e25db4c215dc1d.

Brewer, C.A., McGilloway, J., and Butzler, S.J., 2011, NACIS presentations on terrain inspire Penn State Applied Cartographic Design Course: North American Cartographic Information Society Annual Meeting, Madison, Wisconsin.

Stauffer, A., and Brewer, C.A., 2011, Multiscale terrain representation for *The National Map*: North American Cartographic Information Society Annual Meeting, Madison, Wisconsin.

Brewer, C.A., Buttenfield, B.P., and Stanislawski, L.V., 2011, Choosing between geometry change and display change for multiscale mapping—The role of elimination in design: International Cartographic Conference, Paris, France.

Raposo, P., and Brewer, C.A., 2011, Comparison of topographic map designs for overlay on orthoimage backgrounds: International Cartographic Conference, Paris, France.

Brewer, C.A., Thatcher, J.E., and Butzler, S.J., 2011, Combining varied Federal data sources for multiscale map labeling of populated places and airports for *The National Map* of the United States: International Cartographic Association Commission on Generalisation and Multiple Representation Workshop, Paris, France.

Buttenfield, B.P., Stanislawski, L.V., and Brewer, C.A., 2011, A comparison of star and ladder generalization strategies for intermediate scale processing of USGS National Hydrography Dataset: International Cartographic Association Commission on Generalisation and Multiple Representation Workshop, Paris, France.

Stanislawski, L.V., Buttenfield, B.P., and Brewer, C.A., 2011, Generalization: Center of Excellence for Geospatial Information Science (CEGIS) Annual Research Meeting, Rolla, Missouri.

Brewer, C.A., Stauffer, A., Raposo, P., Butzler, S.J., and Thatcher, J., 2011, Electronic topographic map design: Center of Excellence for Geospatial Information Science (CEGIS) Annual Research Meeting, Rolla, Missouri.

Butzler, S.J., Brewer, C.A., Thatcher, J.E., and Stroh, W.J., 2011, Establishing classification and hierarchy in populated place labeling for multiscale mapping for *The National Map*: *The National Map* Users Conference, Denver, Colorado.

Raposo, P., and Brewer, C.A., 2011, Comparison of topographic map designs for overlay on orthoimage backgrounds: *The National Map* Users Conference, Denver, Colorado.

Brewer, C.A., Hanchett, C.L., Buttenfield, B.P., and Usery, E.L., 2010, Performance of map symbol and label design with format and display resolution options through scale for *The National Map*: AutoCarto 2010, Orlando, Florida.

Stroh, W.J., Butzler, S.J., and Brewer, C.A., 2010, Establishing classification and hierarchy in populated place labeling for multiscale mapping for *The National Map*: AutoCarto 2010, Orlando, Florida.

Wilmer, J.M., and Brewer, C.A., 2010, Application of the radical law in generalization of National Hydrography Data for multiscale mapping: AutoCarto 2010, Orlando, Florida.

Brewer, C.A., Hanchett, C.L., and Buttenfield, B.P., 2010, Design examples for multiscale topographic mapping for *The National Map*: North American Cartographic Information Society Annual Meeting, St. Petersburg, Florida.

Stauffer, A., and Brewer, C.A., 2010, Tapered symbols for NHD flowlines systematically adjusted for dry versus humid zones: North American Cartographic Information Society Annual Meeting, St. Petersburg, Florida.

Butzler, S.J., Stroh, W.J., and Brewer, C.A., 2010, Populated place label classification and hierarchy for multiscale mapping: North American Cartographic Information Society Annual Meeting, St. Petersburg, Florida.

Buttenfield, B.P., Stanislawski, L.V., and Brewer, C.A., 2010, Multiscale representations of rater—Tailoring generalization sequences to specific physiographic regimes: GIScience 2010, Zurich, Switzerland.

Brewer, C.A., Buttenfield, B.P., and Usery, E.L., 2010, Designing USGS topographic mapping for multiscale online use: Geo-Cart' 2010 (New Zealand National Cartographic Conference) and International Cartographic Association (ICA) Symposium on Cartography for Australasia and Oceania, Auckland, New Zealand.

Brewer, C.A., Buttenfield, B.P., and Usery, E.L., 2010, Designing USGS topographic mapping for multiscale online use: Esri International User Conference, San Diego, California.

Brewer, C.A., Buttenfield, B.P., and Stanislawski, L.V., 2010, Progress and rationale for electronic topo map design decisions: Center of Excellence for Geospatial Information Science (CEGIS) Annual Research Meeting, Denver, Colorado.

Hanchett, C.L., and Brewer, C.A., 2010, Multiscale design—ScaleMaster decisions and MXD settings for symbol evaluation: Center of Excellence for Geospatial Information Science (CEGIS) Annual Research Meeting, Denver, Colorado.

Brewer, C.A., and Hanchett, C.L., 2010, Evaluation of map symbols by screen resolution and file format through scale: Center of Excellence for Geospatial Information Science (CEGIS) Annual Research Meeting, Denver, Colorado.

Stauffer, A., and Brewer, C.A., 2010, Tapered symbols for NHD flowlines systematically adjusted for dry versus humid zones: Center of Excellence for Geospatial Information Science (CEGIS) Annual Research Meeting, Denver, Colorado.

Brewer, C.A., 2009, Recommendations for Symbol and label design for multiscale online topographic mapping for *The National Map*: U.S. Geological Survey Headquarters, Reston, Virginia.

Brewer, C.A., Buttenfield, B.P., and Usery, E.L., 2009, Evaluating generalizations of hydrography in differing terrains for *The National Map* of the United States: International Cartographic Conference, Santiago, Chile.

Brewer, C.A., Buttenfield, B.P., and Usery, E.L., 2009, Designing *The National Map* by USGS for multi-scale online use: North American Cartographic Information Society Annual Meeting, Sacramento, California.

Buttenfield, B.P., Brewer, C.A., and Usery, E.L., 2009, Place still matters—Generalizing the National Hydrography Dataset by local terrain and climate: North American Cartographic Information Society Annual Meeting, Sacramento, California.

Brewer, C.A., and Buttenfield, B.P., 2009, Topographic map design to support evaluation of generalization solutions: Center of Excellence for Geospatial Information Science (CEGIS) Annual Research Meeting, Rolla, Missouri.

Wendel, J., Buttenfield, B.P., Anderson-Tarve, C., and Brewer, C.A., 2009, Cartographic generalization by physiographic Region: Association of American Geographers Annual Meeting, Las Vegas, Nevada.

Brewer, C.A., 2008, Redesigned maps: Department of Geography, University of Colorado—Boulder.

Roth, R.E., Stryker, M., and Brewer, C.A., 2008, ScaleMaster.org—Multi-scale mapping made easy: North American Cartographic Information Society Annual Meeting, Missoula, Montana.

Roth, R.E., Stryker, M., and Brewer, C.A., 2008, Typology of multi-scale mapping operators: North American Cartographic Information Society Annual Meeting, Missoula, Montana.

Stryker, M., Roth, R.E., and Brewer, C.A., 2008, ScaleMaster.org—Illustrating and constructing the multi-scale mapping process: GIScience 2008, Park City, Utah.

Roth, R.E., Stryker, M., and Brewer, C.A., 2008, Typology of multi-scale mapping operator: GIScience 2008, Park City, Utah.

Brewer, C.A., and Akella, M.K., 2008, Multi-resolution multi-scale topographic map design—Toward a new look for *The National Map*: AutoCarto 2008, Shepherdstown, West Virginia.

Brewer, C.A., and Akella, M.K., 2008, Multi-resolution multi-scale topographic map design: Esri International User Conference, San Diego, California.

Brewer, C.A., 2008, Electronic topographic map design: Center of Excellence for Geospatial Information Science (CEGIS) Annual Research Meeting, Rolla, Missouri.

Publications Related to CEGIS Generalization Initiative (2007–2012)

Barbara Buttenfield

(NOTE: Barbara Buttenfield and Cindy Brewer joined CEGIS as Faculty Affiliates in 2008, and publications on generalization prior to 2008 were funded by Esri not USGS. As a consequence, they are not listed here. Larry Stanislawski's publication record dates back through 2007. Cindy may have publications on the E-TOPO Design project in addition to those listed in this document.)

Books

Buttenfield, B.P. and Mackaness, W.A. eds., Generalization and spatial sata Integration (in preparation).

Articles in Refereed Journals

Buttenfield, B.P., Stanislawski, L.V., and Brewer, C.A., 2011, Adapting generalization tools to physiographic diversity for the USGS National Hydrography Dataset: Cartography and GIS, v. 38, no. 3, p. 289–301.

Stanislawski, L.V., and Buttenfield, B.P., 2011, Hydrographic generalization tailored to dry dountainous regions: Cartography and GIS, v. 38, no. 2, p. 117–125.

Anderson-Tarver, C., Leyk, S., and Buttenfield, B.P., 2011, Fuzzy modeling of geometric textures for identifying archipelagos in area-patch generalization: Cartography and GIS, v. 38, no. 2, p. 137–146.

Brewer, C.A., and Buttenfield, B.P., 2010, Mastering map scale—Balancing workloads using display and geometry change in multi-scale mapping: Geoinformatica, v. 14, no. 2, p. 221–239.

Wendel, J., Buttenfield, B.P., and Smith, J., 2009, Spatializing a GIS software toolbox: Kartographische Nachrichten, vol. 5, p. 257–263.

Stanislawski, L.V., 2009, Feature pruning by upstream drainage area to support automated generalization of the United States National Hydrography Dataset: Computers, Environment, and Urban Systems, v. 33, no. 5, p. 325–333.

Refereed Conference Proceedings

Stanislawski, L.V., Doumbouya, A.T., and Miller-Corbett, C.D., 2012, Mapping natural variability in drainage density for the coterminous United States to support hydrologic generalization [abs.]: GIS in the Rockies, Denver, Colorado, September 2012.

Stanislawski, L.V., Doumbouya, A.T., Miller-Corbett, C.D., Buttenfield, B.P., and Arundel-Murin, S.T., 2012, Scaling stream densities for hydrologic generalization [abs.]: Proceedings, short paper, GIScience 2012, Columbus, Ohio, September 2012,

Stanislawski, L.V., Briat, M.O., Punt, E., Howard, M., Brewer, C.A., and Buttenfield, B.P., 2012, Density stratified thinning of road networks to support automated generalization for *The National Map* [abs.]: Proceedings: Workshop of the International Cartographic Association Commission on Generalisation and Multiple Representation, 15th, Istanbul, Turkey, September 2012.

Wolf, E.B., and Buttenfield, B.P., 2012, Aggregating data quality metrics for item level metadata [abs.]: Proceedings, Auto-Carto 12, Columbus, Ohio, September 2012.

Stauffer, A.J., Buttenfield, B.P., and Stanislawski, L.V., 2012, Effects of generalization on DEM resolution [abs.]: Proceedings, Auto-Carto 12, Columbus, Ohio, September 2012.

Stanislawski, L.V., Raposo, P., Howard, M., and Buttenfield, B.P., 2012, Automated metric assessment of line simplification in humid landscapes [abs.]: Proceedings, Auto-Carto 12, Columbus, Ohio, September 2012.

Brewer, C.A., Stanislawski, L.V., Buttenfield, B.P., Raposo, P., Sparks, K., and Howard, M., 2012, Multi-scale design for *The National Map* of the United States—Roads, populated places, boundaries and landcover [abs.]: Proceedings, Auto-Carto 12, Columbus, Ohio, September 2012.

Anderson-Tarver, C., Gleason, M., Buttenfield, B.P., and Stanislawski, L.V., 2012, Automated centerline delineation to enrich the National Hydrography Dataset *in* Xiao, N., Kwan, M.P., and Lin, H., eds., Lecture notes in computer science vol. 7478: GIScience 2012, p. 15–28.

Buttenfield, B.P., Stanislawski, L.V., and Brewer, C.A., 2011, A comparison of star and ladder strategies for intermediate scale processing of USGS National Hydrography Dataset: Proceedings, Workshop of the International Cartographic Association Commission on Generalisation and Multiple Representation, 14th, Paris, France, July 2011.

Stanislawski, L.V., and Buttenfield, B.P., 2011, A raster alternative for partitioning line densities to support sutomated carto-graphicgeneralization: Proceedings, Workshop of the International Cartographic Association Commission on Generalisa-tion and Multiple Representation, 14th, Paris, France, July 2011.

Stanislawski, L.V., and Savino, S., 2011, Pruning of hydrographic networks—A comparison of two approaches: Proceedings, Workshop of the International Cartographic Association/International Society for Photogrammetry and Remote Sensing on Generalisation and Multiple Representation, 14th, Paris, France, July 2011.

Anderson-Tarver, C., and Buttenfield, B.P., Stanislawski, L.V., and Koontz, J., 2011, Automated delineation of stream centerlines for the USGS National Hydrography Dataset: Proceedings, International Cartographic Congress, Advances in Cartography and GIScience, 25th, Paris, France, July 2011, v. 1. [Lecture notes *in* Geoinformation and Cartography, p. 409–423.]

Wendel, J., and Buttenfield, B.P., 2011, Flexible characterization of cartographic generalization resources for an online self-organizing catalog: Proceedings, International Cartographic Congress, 25th, Paris, France, July 2011.

Brewer, C.A., Buttenfield, B.P., and Stanislawski, L.V, 2011, Choosing between geometry change and display change for multiscale mapping—The role of elimination in design: Proceedings, Workshop of the International Cartographic Associa-tion Commission on Generalisation and Multiple Representation, 14th, Paris, France, July 2011.

Stanislawski, L.V., and Buttenfield, B.P., 2010, Hydrographic feature generalization in dry mountainous terrain: Proceedings, AutoCarto 2010, Orlando, Florida, November 2010.

Stanislawski, L.V., Finn, M.P., and Buttenfield, B.P., 2010, Integrating hydrographic generalization over multiple physio-graphic regimes. Chapter *in* Generalization and Data Integration book, compiled for CEGIS International Symposium on Generalization and Data Integration, Boulder, Colorado, June 2010.

Anderson-Tarver, C., Leyk, S., and Buttenfield, B.P., 2010, Identifying vector feature textures using fuzzy sets: Proceedings, AutoCarto 2010, Orlando, Florida, November 2010.

Brewer, C.A., Hanchett, C.L., Buttenfield, B.P., and Usery, E.L., 2010, Performance of map symbol and label design with format and display resolution options through scale for *The National Map*: Proceedings, AutoCarto 2010, Orlando, Florida, November 2010.

Buttenfield, B.P., Stanislawski, L.V., and Brewer, C.A., 2010, Multiscale representations of water—Tailoring generalization sequences to specific physiographic regimes: Proceedings, short paper, GIScience 2010, Zurich, Switzerland, September 2010.

Wendel, J., and Buttenfield, B. P., 2010, Formalizing guidelines for building self-organizing maps: Proceedings, short paper, GIScience 2010, Zurich, Switzerland, September 2010.

Stanislawski, L.V., Buttenfield, B.P. and Samaranayake, V.A., 2010, Automated metric assessment of hydrographic feature generalization through bootstrapping: Proceedings, International Cartographic Association Symposium on Multiple Rep-resentations and Map Generalization, 13th, Zurich, Switzerland, September 2010.

Brewer, C.A., Buttenfield, B.P., and Usery, E.L., 2009, Evaluating generalizations of hydrography in differing terrains for *The National Map* of the United States: Proceedings, International Cartographic Conference, Santiago, Chile, November 2009.

Stanislawski, L.V., Buttenfield, B.P., Finn, M.P., and Roth, K., 2009, Stratified database pruning to support local density variations in automated generalization of the United States National Hydrography Dataset: Proceedings, International Cartographic Conference, Santiago, Chile, November 2009.

Wolf, E.B., and Buttenfield, B.P., 2008, Dimensional collapse and airports in multi-scale mapping: Proceedings, AutoCarto 2008, Shephardstown, West Virginia, September 2008.

Wendel, J., Buttenfield, B.P., Viger, R., and Smith, J., 2008, Characterizing hydrology commands—Spatialization with SOM mapping: Proceedings, GIScience 2008, Park City, Utah, September 2008.

Stanislawski, L.V., 2008, Development of a knowledge-based network pruning strategy for automated generalisation of the United States National Hydrography Dataset: Proceedings, Workshop of the International Cartographic Association on Generalisation and Multiple Representation, 11th, Montpellier, France, June 2008.

Invited Keynotes, Lectures, and Colloquia

2011

Buttenfield, B.P., 2011, Multiple representations of geospatial data—A cartographic search for the Holy Grail?: *The National Map* Users Conference, Denver Colorado, May 2011.

2010

Buttenfield, B.P., 2010, Mapping water with the best intentions: Department of Geography, Penn State University.

Buttenfield, B.P., 2010, Generalization and data integration: University of Zurich, Switzerland.

Conference Presentations Not Published in Proceedings or Journal Articles

2012

Buttenfield, B.P., Gleason, M., and Tarver, C., 2012, Automatic delineation of centerlines and stream braids for cartographic generalization: North American Cartographic Information Society Annual Meeting (NACIS 32), Portland, Oregon, October 2012.

Wendel, J., Buttenfield, B.P., and Stanislawski, L.V., 2012, Comparison of unsupervised learning algorithms for physiographic classification of U.S. landscape types: Annual Meetings of the Association of American Geographers, New York City, February 2012.

Stanislawski, L.V., 2012, Overview of CEGIS NHD and Transportation generalization tools for grid-computing application: CEGIS visit to National Center for Supercomputing Applications at University of Illinois–Champaign, Champaign-Urbana Illinois, February 2012.

2011

Gleason, M.J., Pitlick, J., and Buttenfield, B.P., 2011, Filtering raw terrestrial laser scanning data for more efficient and accurate use in geomorphologic modeling: American Geophysical Union Annual Meetings, San Francisco, California, December 2011.

Stanislawski, L.V., Finelli, E., Doumbouya, A., and Buttenfield, B.P., 2011, Metric assessment of NHD cartographic generalization supporting 1:24,000 USGS digital topographic maps for New Jersey: USGS GIS Workshop: Denver, Colorado, May 2011.

Finelli, E.L., Bates, A.T., Stanislawski, L.V., and Buttenfield, B.P., 2011, National Hydrography Dataset Generalization case study—From local resolution New Jersey NHD to 1:24,000-scale: USGS GIS Workshop: Denver, Colorado, May 2011.

Buttenfield, B.P., 2011, Automated methods for simplifying surface water features: flowlines, waterbodies and centerlines: USGS Workshop on Cartographic Generalization and Concurrent Processing, Rolla, Missouri, October 2011. (web presentation).

Stanislawski, L.V., 2011, Estimating 1:24,000-scale drainage density for the coterminous United States using Elevation-derived streams: USGS Workshop on Cartographic Generalization and Concurrent Processing, Rolla, Missouri, October 2011. (web presentation).

Stanislawski, L.V., 2011, Partitioning Line densities to support automated cartographic generalization: USGS Workshop on Cartographic Generalization and Concurrent Processing, Rolla, Missouri, October 2011. (web presentation).

Stanislawski, L.V., 2011, Overview of Procedures to prune high-resolution NHD: USGS Workshop on Cartographic Generalization and Concurrent Processing, Rolla, Missouri, October 2011. (web presentation).

Stanislawski, L.V., 2011, Overview of CEGIS Generalization research on best practices transportation data: USGS Workshop on Cartographic Generalization and Concurrent Processing, Rolla, Missouri, October 17. (web presentation).

Stanislawski, L.V., 2011, Landscape Classification to support automated generalization: USGS Workshop on Cartographic Generalization and Concurrent Processing, Rolla, Missouri, October 2011. (web presentation).

Stanislawski, L.V., 2011, Catchment and upstream drainage area processing for enriching the NHD for generalization: USGS Workshop on Cartographic Generalization and Concurrent Processing, Rolla, Missouri, October 2011. (web presentation).

Howard, M., and Stanislawski, L.V., 2011, Average Segment length within landscape classes of NHD subbasins: USGS Workshop on Cartographic Generalization and Concurrent Processing, Rolla, Missouri, October 2011. (web presentation).

Stanislawski, L.V., 2011, Review of coefficient of line correspondence and coefficient of area correspondence for hydrography validation: USGS Workshop on Cartographic Generalization and Concurrent Processing, Rolla, Missouri, October 2011. (web presentation).

Finelli, E., 2011, National Map—US Topo Requirements: generalized local resolution NHD to 1:24,000: USGS Workshop on Cartographic Generalization and Concurrent Processing, Rolla, Missouri, October 2011. (web presentation).

Buttenfield, B.P., and Gleason, M., 2011, Automatic identification of islands in the National Hydrography Dataset: USGS Workshop on Cartographic Generalization and Concurrent Processing, Rolla, Missouri, 2011. (web presentation).

Buttenfield, B.P. and Stanislawski, L.V., 2011, Generalization for *The National Map*: USGS-CEGIS "All-Hands" Annual Research Meeting, Rolla, Missouri, June 2011.

2010

Brewer, C.A., Buttenfield, B.P., and E.L., Usery, 2010, Designing USGS Topographic mapping for multiscale online use: Esri User Conference, San Diego, California, July 2010.

Brewer, C.A., Buttenfield, B.P., and E.L., Usery, 2010, Designing USGS Topographic mapping for multiscale online use: International Cartographic Symposium on Cartography for Australasia and Oceania (GeoCart 2010), Auckland, New Zealand, September 2010.

Buttenfield, B.P., Stanislawski, L.V., and Brewer, C.A., 2010, Generalization to support *The National Map*: USGS-CEGIS "All-Hands" Annual Research Meeting, Denver, Colorado, June. 2010.

Brewer, C.A., B.P., Buttenfield, and Stanislawski, L.V., 2010, Progress on electronic topo map design decisions: USGS-CEGIS "All-Hands" Annual Research Meeting, Denver, Colorado, June 2010.

Brewer, C.A., Hanchett, C.L., Buttenfield, B.P., and Stanislawski, L.V., 2010, Evaluation of map symbols by screen resolution and file format through scale: USGS-CEGIS "All-Hands" Annual Research Meeting, Denver, Colorado, June 2010.

Wendel, J., and Buttenfield, B.P., 2010, Guidelines for self-organizing maps: Annual Meetings Association of American Geographers, Washington D.C., April 2010.

Anderson-Tarver, C., and Buttenfield, B.P., 2010, Generalizing a swamp-marsh database using texture: Annual Meetings Association of American Geographers, Washington D.C., April 2010.

Stanislawski, L.V., 2010, Cluster Processing for enriching the National Hydrography Dataset for Automated Generalization: University of Illinois–Champaign, Cyberinfrastructure and Geospatial Information Laboratory, visit to USGS, Rolla, Missouri, March 2010.

2009

Buttenfield, B.P., Brewer, C.A., and Usery, E.L., 2009, Place still matters—Generalizing the National Hydrography Dataset by local terrain and climate: North American Cartographic Information Society (NACIS 29), Sacramento, California, October 2009.

Brewer, C.A., Buttenfield, B.P., and Usery, E.L., 2009, Designing *The National Map* produced by USGS for multi-scale online use: North American Cartographic Information Society (NACIS 29), Sacramento, California, October 2009.

Buttenfield, B.P., Stanislawski, L.V., and Brewer, C.A., 2009, NHD generalization and multiscale topographic map design: USGS Center for Excellence "All-Hands" Annual Research Meeting, Rolla, Missouri, August 2009.

Stanislawski, L.V., 2009, An automated approach to compare generalized hydrographic network features to a benchmark dataset: Dagstuhl Seminar on Generalization of Spatial Information, Schloss-Dagstuhl, Germany, April 2009.

Wendel, J., Buttenfield, B.P., Anderson-Tarver, C., and Brewer, C.A., 2009, Cartographic generalization by physiographic region: Annual Meetings Association of American Geographers, Las Vegas, Nevada, April 2009.

2008

Buttenfield, B.P., 2008, Hydrographic generalization—Problems to solve for *The National Map*: USGS Center for Excellence "All-Hands" Annual Research Meeting, Rolla, Missouri, 2008.

Stanislawski, L.V., 2008, Generalization of primary data themes for *The National Map*: USGS CEGIS "All-Hands" Annual Research Meeting, Rolla, Missouri, 2008.

Viger, R., and Buttenfield, B.P., 2008, Semantics for integrating hydrologic models: USGS Symposium on GIS Research, USGS Headquarters, Reston, Virginia, September 2008.

Wendel, J., Buttenfield, B.P., Viger, R., and Smith, J., 2008, Spatializing GIS commands with self-organizing maps: Annual Meetings Association of American Geographers, Boston, Massachusetts, April 2008.

Stanislawski, L.V., and Schnarr III, O.C., 2008, Implementation of an automated network pruning strategy for generalization of the National Hydrography Dataset: Annual Meetings Association of American Geographers, Boston, Massachusetts. April 2008.

2007

Stanislawski, L.V., Finn, M., Barnes, M., and Usery, E.L., 2007, Assessment of a rapid approach for estimating catchment areas for surface drainage lines: American Congress on Survey and Mapping–Illinois Professional Land Surveyors Association–Missouri Society of Professional Surveyors (ACSM-IPLSA-MSPS) 2007, St. Louis, Missouri, March 2007.

Chair of the following Ph.D. Committees with Research Directly Related to CEGIS Research

Wendel, Jochen, University of. Colorado—Boulder (entered the program Fall 2007)
Explicit and Implicit Indexing Schemas for Multiple Data Types of Online Generalization
Resources; Dissertation defense planned January 2013

Supervised Master's degrees (University of Colorado)

Stauffer, Andrew   (ongoing)   Impacts of Iterative Filtering on Terrain Resolution;
                                                             Entered the program August 2011
Gleason, Michael   (ongoing)   Filtering TLIDAR Point Clouds for DEM Interpolation;
Thesis defense November 28, 2012

Anderson-Tarver, Chris (February 2010)   Generalizing a Swamp-Marsh Database Using Texture

Generalization

Larry Stanislawski

Journal Articles

Brewer, C.A., Stanislawski, L.V., Buttenfield, B.P., Raposo, P., Sparks, K., and Howard, M.A., 2012, Multiscale design of thinned road networks for *The National Map* of the United States: Cartography and Geographic Information Science (submitted; under review).

Buttenfield, B.P., Stanislawski, L.V., and Brewer, C.A., 2011, Adapting generalization tools to physiographic diversity for the United States National Hydrography Dataset: Cartography and Geographic Information Science, v. 38, no. 3, p. 289–301.

Stanislawski, L.V., and Buttenfield, B.P., 2011, Hydrographic generalization tailored to dry mountainous regions: Cartography and Geographic Information Science, v. 38, no. 2, p.117–125.

Stanislawski, L.V., 2009, Feature pruning by upstream drainage area to support automated generalization of the United States National Hydrography Dataset: Computers, Environment, and Urban Systems, v. 33, no. 5, p.325–333.

Proceedings and Workshop Papers (peer-reviewed)

Buttenfield, B.P., Stanislawski, L.V., Anderson-Tarver, C., and Gleason, M.J., 2012, Automatic enrichment of stream networks with primary paths for sse in the United States National Atlas: Proceedings, International Cartographic Congress, 26th, Dresden, Germany, August 2013. (submitted November 14, 2012; under review).

Stanislawski, L.V., Buttenfield, B.P., and Brewer, C.A., 2012, Integration metrics for cartographic generalization—Assessment of 1:1000,000 scale hydrography and terrain: Proceedings, International Cartographic Congress, 26th, Dresden, Germany, August 2013. (submitted November 14, 2012; under review).

Brewer, C.A., Stanislawski, L.V., and Buttenfield, B.P., 2012, Labeling through scale using hierarchies of thinned Road networks for design of *The National Map* of the United States: Proceedings, International Cartographic Congress, 26th, Dresden, Germany, August 2012. (submitted November 14, 2012; under review).

Anderson-Tarver, C., Gleason, M., Buttenfield, B.P., and Stanislawski, L.V., 2012, Automated centerline delineation to enrich the National Hydrography Dataset: International Conference on Geographic Information Science, 7th, September 2012, Columbus, Ohio, Lecture Notes in Computer Science, v. 7478, p.15–28.

Stanislawski, L.V., Briat, M., Punt, E., Howard, M., Brewer, C.A., and Buttenfield, B.P., 2012, Density stratified thinning of road networks to support automated generalization of *The National Map*: Workshop of the International Cartographic Association on Generalization, 15th, Istanbul, Turkey, September 2012.

Stanislawski, L.V., Doumbouya, A.T., Miller-Corbett, C.D., Buttenfield, B.P. and Arundel-Murin, S.T., 2012, Scaling stream densities for hydrologic generalizations: International Conference on Geographic Information Science, 7th, Columbus, Ohio, September 2012.

Anderson-Tarver, C., Buttenfield, B.P., Stanislawski, L.V., and Koontz, J., 2012, Automated delineation of stream centerlines for the USGS National Hydrography Dataset: Proceedings, International Cartographic Conference, 25th, Paris, France, July 2011, v. 1, [Lecture notes *in* Geoinformation and Cartography, p. 409–423.]

Brewer, C.A., Buttenfield, B.P., and Stanislawski, L.V., 2011, Choosing between geometry change and display change for multiscale mapping—The role of elimination in design: Workshop of the International Cartographic Association/International Society for Photogrammetry and Remote Sensing on Generalization and Multiple Representations, 14th, Paris, France, June/July 2011.

Buttenfield, B.P., Stanislawski, L.V., and Brewer, C.A., 2011, A comparison of star and ladder strategies for intermediate scale processing of USGS National Hydrography Dataset: Workshop of the International Cartographic Association/International Society for Photogrammetry and Remote Sensing on Generalization and Multiple Representations, 14th, Paris, France, June/July 2011.

Stanislawski, L.V., and Savino, S., 2011, Pruning of hydrographic networks: a comparison of two approaches: Workshop of the International Cartographic Association/International Society for Photogrammetry and Remote Sensing on Generalization and Multiple Representations, 14th, Paris, France, June/July 2011.

Stanislawski, L.V., and Buttenfield, B.P., 2011, A raster alternative for partitioning line densities to support automated cartographic generalization: International Cartographic Conference, 25th, Paris, France, July 2011.

Buttenfield, B.P., and Stanislawski, L.V., 2010, Multiscale representations of water—Tailoring generalization sequences to specific physiographic regimes: International Conference on Geographic Information Science, 6th, Zurich, Switzerland, September 2010.

Stanislawski, L.V., Buttenfield, B.P., and Samaranayake, V.A., 2010, Automated metric assessment of hydrographic feature generalization through bootstrapping: Workshop of the International Cartographic Association on Generalization and Multiple Representations, 12th, Zurich, Switzerland, September, 2010.

Stanislawski, L.V., Buttenfield, B.P., Finn, M.P., and Roth, K., 2009, Stratified database pruning to support local density variations in automated generalization of the United States National Hydrography Dataset: International Cartographic Conference, 24th, Santiago, Chile, November 2009.

Stanislawski, L.V., 2008, Development of a knowledge-based network pruning strategy for automated generalisation of the United States National Hydrography Dataset: Workshop of the International Cartographic Association on Generalisation and Multiple Representations, 11th, Montpellier, France, June 2008.

Proceedings and Workshop Papers (not peer-reviewed)

Brewer, C.A., Stanislawski, L.V., Buttenfield, B.P., Raposo, P., Sparks, K.A., and Howard, M., 2012, Multiscale design for *The National Map* of the United States—Road thinning for topographic Mapping: AutoCarto 2012, Columbus, Ohio, September 2012.

Stanislawski, L.V., Raposo, P., Howard, M., and Buttenfield, B.P., 2012, Automated metric assessment of line simplification in humid landscapes: AutoCarto 2012, Columbus, Ohio, September 2012.

Stauffer, A., Buttenfield, B.P., and Stanislawski, L.V., 2012, Effects of generalization on DEM resolution: AutoCarto 2012, Columbus, Ohio, September 2012.

Stanislawski, L.V., Finn, M.P., and Buttenfield, B.P., 2010, Integrating hydrographic generalization over multiple physiographic regimes. Chapter *in* Generalization and Data Integration book, compiled for CEGIS International Symposium on Generalization and Data Integration, Boulder, Colorado, June 2010.

Stanislawski, L.V., Buttenfield, B.P., 2010, Hydrographic feature generalization in dry mountainous terrain: AutoCarto 2010, Orlando, Florida, November 2010.

Stanislawski, L.V., Finn, M., Barnes, M., and Usery, E.L., 2007, Assessment of a rapid approach for estimating catchment areas for surface drainage lines. American Congress on Surveying and Mapping–Illinois Professional Land Surveyors Association–Missouri Society of Professional Surveyors, (ACSM-IPLSA-MSPS 2007): St. Louis, Missouri, March 2007.

Stanislawski, L.V., Finn, M., Usery, E.L., and Robinette, P. M., 2007, Development of a blunder detection approach for automated point matching during vector to image data integration: American Society of Photogrammetry and Remote Sensing (ASPRS) 2007 Annual Conference, Tampa, Florida, May 2007.

Stanislawski, L.V., Finn, M., Starbuck, M., Usery, E.L., and Turley, P., 2006, Estimation of accumulated upstream drainage values in braided streams using augmented directed graphs: AutoCarto 2006, Vancouver, Washington, June 2006.

Stanislawski, L.V., Starbuck, M., Finn, M., and Usery, E.L., 2005, Generalization for *The National Map* with emphasis on the National Hydrography Dataset: Esri International User Conference 2005, San Diego, California, July 2005.

Presentations

2012

Buttenfield, B.P., Gleason, M.J., and Anderson-Tarver, C., 2012, Automatic delineation of primary channels through braided stream networks for cartographic generalization: North American Cartographic Information Society (NACIS 2012), Portland, Oregon, October 2012.

Anderson-Tarver, C., Gleason, M., Buttenfield, B.P., and Stanislawski, L.V., 2012, Automated centerline delineation to enrich the National Hydrography Dataset: Seventh International Conference on Geographic Information Science, Columbus, Ohio, September 2012.

Brewer, C.A., Stanislawski, L.V., Buttenfield, B.P., Raposo, P., Sparks, K.A., and Howard, M., 2012, Multiscale design for *The National Map* of the United States—Road thinning for topographic mapping: AutoCarto 2012, Columbus, Ohio, September 2012,

Stanislawski, L.V., 2012, Overview of CEGIS NHD and Transportation generalization tools for grid-computing application: CEGIS visit to National Center for Supercomputing Applications at the University of Illinois–Champaign, Champaign-Urbana, Illinois, February 2012.

Stanislawski, L.V., Briat, M., Punt, E., Howard, M., Brewer, C.A., and Buttenfield, B.P., 2012, Density stratified thinning of road networks to support automated generalization of *The National Map*: International Cartographic Association (ICA) Workshop on Generalization, 15th, Istanbul, Turkey, September 2012.

Stanislawski, L.V., Doumbouya, A.T., Miller-Corbett, C.D., Buttenfield, B.P., and Arundel-Murin, S.T., 2012, Scaling stream densities for hydrologic generalizations: International Conference on Geographic Information Science, 7th, Columbus, Ohio, September 2012.

Stanislawski, L.V., Doumbouya, A.T., and Miller-Corbett, C.D., 2012, Mapping natural variability in drainage density for the coterminous United States to support hydrologic generalization: GIS in the Rockies 2012, Denver, Colorado, September 2012.

Stanislawski, L.V., Raposo, P., Howard, M., and Buttenfield, B.P., 2012, Automated metric assessment of line simplification in humid landscapes: AutoCarto 2012, Columbus, Ohio, September 2012.

Stauffer, A., Buttenfield, B.P., and Stanislawski, L.V., 2012, Effects of generalization on DEM resolution: AutoCarto 2012, Columbus, Ohio, September 2012.

Wendel, J., Buttenfield, B.P., and Stanislawski, L., 2012, Comparison of unsupervised learning algorithms for physiographic classification of the United States landscape types: Annual Meetings of the Association of American Geographers. New York, New York, February 2012.

2011

Gleason, M.J., Pitlick, J., and Buttenfield, B.P., 2011, Filtering raw terrestrial laser scanning data for more efficient and accurate Use in Geomorphologic Modeling: American Geophysical Union Annual Meetings, San Francisco, California, December 2011.

Anderson-Tarver, C., Buttenfield, B.P., Stanislawski, L.V., and Koontz, J., 2011, Automated delineation of stream centerlines for the USGS National Hydrography Dataset: Proceedings, International Cartographic Conference, 25th, Paris, France, July 2011, v. 1. [Lecture notes *in* Geoinformation and Cartography, p. 409–423.]

Brewer, C.A., Buttenfield, B.P., and Stanislawski, L.V., 2011, Choosing between geometry change and display change for multi-scale mapping—The role of elimination in design: International Cartographic Association/American Society for Photogrammetry and Remote Sensing (ICA/ASPRS) workshop on Generalization and Multiple Representations, 14th, Paris, France, June/July 2011.

Buttenfield, B.P., Stanislawski, L.V., and Brewer, C.A., 2011, A comparison of star and ladder strategies for intermediate scale processing of USGS National Hydrography Dataset: International Cartographic Association/American Society for Photogrammetry and Remote Sensing (ICA/ASPRS) Paris, France, June/July 2011.

Buttenfield, B.P., and Stanislawski, L.V., 2011, Generalization for *The National Map*: USGS-CEGIS "All-Hands" Annual Research Meeting, Rolla, Missouri, June 2011.

Finelli, E.L., Bates, A.T., Stanislawski, L.V., and Buttenfield, B.P., 2011, National Hydrography Dataset generalization case study—From local resolution New Jersey NHD to 1:24,000-Scale: USGS GIS Workshop, Denver, Colorado, May 2011.

Howard, M., and Stanislawski, L.V., 2011, Average segment length within landscape classes of NHD subbasins: USGS Workshop on Cartographic Generalization and Concurrent Processing, Rolla, Missouri, October 2011. (web presentation).

Stanislawski, L.V., Finelli, E., Doumbouya, A., and Buttenfield, B.P., 2011, Metric Assessment of NHD cartographic generalization supporting 1:24,000 USGS digital topographic maps for New Jersey: USGS GIS Workshop. Denver, Colorado, May 2011.

Stanislawski, L.V., and Savino, S., 2011, Pruning of hydrographic networks—A comparison of two approaches: International Cartographic Association/American Society for Photogrammetry and Remote Sensing (ICA/ASPRS), 14th, workshop on Generalization and Multiple Representations, Paris, France, June/July 2011.

Stanislawski, L.V., and Buttenfield, B.P., 2011, A raster alternative for partitioning line densities to support automated cartographic generalization: International Cartographic Conference, 25th, Paris, France, July 2011.

Stanislawski, L.V., 2011, Estimating 1:24,000-scale drainage density for the coterminous United States using elevation-derived streams: USGS workshop on Cartographic Generalization and Concurrent Processing, Rolla, Missouri, October 2011. (web presentation).

Stanislawski, L.V., 2011, Partitioning line densities to support automated cartographic generalization: USGS workshop on Cartographic Generalization and Concurrent Processing, Rolla, Missouri, October 2011. (web presentation).

Stanislawski, L.V., 2011, Overview of procedures to prune high-resolution NHD: USGS workshop on Cartographic Generalization and Concurrent Processing, Rolla, Missouri, October 2011. (web presentation).

Stanislawski, L.V., 2011, Overview of CEGIS Generalization research on best practices transportation data: USGS workshop on Cartographic Generalization and Concurrent Processing, Rolla, Missouri, October 2011. (web presentation).

Stanislawski, L.V., 2011, Landscape classification to support automated generalization: USGS workshop on Cartographic Generalization and Concurrent Processing, Rolla, Missouri, October 2011. (web presentation).

Stanislawski, L.V., 2011, Catchment and upstream drainage area processing for enriching the NHD for generalization: USGS workshop on Cartographic Generalization and Concurrent Processing, Rolla, Missouri, October 2011. (web presentation).

Stanislawski, L.V., 2011, Review of Coefficient of Line Correspondence and Coefficient of Area Correspondence for Hydrography validation: USGS Workshop on Cartographic Generalization and Concurrent Processing, Rolla, Missouri, October 2011. (web presentation).

2010

Buttenfield, B.P., Stanislawski, L.V., and Brewer, C.A., 2010, Generalization to support *The National Map*: USGS-CEGIS "All-Hands" Annual Research Meeting, Denver, Colorado, June 2010.

Buttenfield, B.P., and Stanislawski, L.V., 2010, Multiscale representations of water—Tailoring generalization sequences to specific physiographic regimes: International Conference on Geographic Information Science, 6th, Zurich, Switzerland, September 2010.

Brewer, C.A., Buttenfield, B.P., and Stanislawski, L., 2010, Progress on electronic topo map design decisions: USGS-CEGIS "All-Hands" Annual Research Meeting, Denver, Colorado, June 2010.

Brewer, C.A., Hanchett, C.L., Buttenfield, B.P., and Stanislawski, L., 2010, Evaluation of map symbols by screen resolution and file format through scale: USGS-CEGIS "All-Hands" Annual Research Meeting, Denver, Colorado, June 2010.

Stanislawski, L.V., Buttenfield, B.P., 2010, Hydrographic feature generalization in dry mountainous terrain: AutoCarto 2010, Orlando, Florida, November 2010.

Stanislawski, L.V., Buttenfield, B.P., and Samaranayake, V.A., 2010, Automated metric assessment of hydrographic feature generalization through bootstrapping: International Cartographic Association (ICA) Workshop on Generalization and Multiple Representations, 12th, Zurich, Switzerland, September 2010.

Stanislawski, L.V., 2010, Cluster Processing for enriching the national hydrography dataset for automated generalization: University of Illinois–Champaign, cyberinfrastructure and geospatial information laboratory visit to USGS, Rolla, Missouri, March 2010.

2009

Stanislawski, L.V., Buttenfield, B.P., Finn, M.P., and Roth, K., 2009, Stratified database pruning to support local density variations in automated generalization of the United States National Hydrography Dataset: International Cartographic Conference, 24th, Santiago, Chile, November 2009.

Stanislawski, L.V., 2009, An automated approach to compare generalized hydrographic network features to a benchmark dataset: Dagstuhl seminar on generalization of spatial information, Schloss-Dagstuhl, Germany, April 2009.

2008

Stanislawski, L.V., and Schnarr III, O.C., 2008, Implementation of an automated network pruning strategy for generalization of the National Hydrography Dataset: Association of American Geographers (AAG) 2008 Annual Meeting, Boston, Massachusetts, April 2008.

Stanislawski, L.V., 2008, Development of a knowledge-based network pruning strategy for automated generalisation of the United States National Hydrography Dataset: International Cartographic Association (ICA) Workshop on Generalisation and Multiple Representation, 11th, Montpellier, France, June 2008.

2007

Stanislawski, L.V., Finn, M., Barnes, M., and Usery, E.L., 2007, Assessment of a rapid approach for estimating catchment areas for surface drainage lines: American Congress on Survey and Mapping–Illinois Professional Land Surveyors Association–Missouri Society of Professional Surveyors (ACSM-IPLSA-MSPS 2007): St. Louis, Missouri. March 2007.

Stanislawski, L.V., Finn, M., Usery, E.L., and Robinette, P. M.,. 2007, Development of a blunder detection approach for automated point matching during vector to image data integration: American Society for Photogrammetry and Remote Sensing (ASPRS) 2007 Annual Conference, Tampa, Florida, May 2007.

2006

Stanislawski, L.V., Finn, M., Starbuck, M., Usery, E.L., and Turley, P., 2006, Estimation of accumulated upstream drainage values in braided streams using augmented directed graphs: AutoCarto 2006, Vancouver, Washington, June 2006.

2005

Stanislawski, L.V., Starbuck, M., Finn, M. and Usery, E.L., 2005, Generalization for *The National Map* with emphasis on the National Hydrography Dataset: Esri International User Conference 2005, San Diego, California, July 2005.

Publications and Presentation 2007–2012

Data Integration

Integration of Roads and Images (includes some items that pre-date CEGIS and 2007, but were part of the Data Integration project)

E. Lynn Usery, Michael Finn and others

Presentations

2009

Usery, E.L., 2009, Geospatial data integration—A review and a USGS approach: China-U.S. Roundtable on Scientific Data Cooperation, Qingdao, China.

Usery, E.L., 2009, Geospatial Data Integration—A review and a USGS approach: University of Missouri–Kansas City.

2007

Usery, E.L., 2007. Data Integration for *The National Map*: University of Missouri-Rolla.

Stanislawski, L., Finn, M.P., Usery, E.L., and Robinette, P.L., 2007, Development of a blunder detection approach for automated point matching during vector to image data Integration: Proceedings, American Society for Photogrammetry and Remote Sensing Annual Conference, Tampa, Florida, 2007.

2003

Usery, E.L., 2003, Data Integration of layers and features for *The National Map*: American Congress on Surveying and Mapping, Phoenix, Arizona.

Publications

Weaver, B., 2004, Data and institutional integration across spatial scales for *The National Ma*p: Unpublished master's Thesis, University of Georgia.

Usery, E.L., Finn, M.P., Weaver, B., Starbuck, M., and Jaromack, G.M., 2004, Integration of *The National Map*: International Society for Photogrammetry and Remote Sensing, Istanbul, Turkey, presented by M.P. Finn, August, 2004.

Usery, E.L., Finn, M.P., and Starbuck, M., 2009, Data layer integration for *The National Map* of The United States: Cartographic Perspectives, v. 62, p. 28–41.

Usery, E.L., 2012, Generalization and data integration (GDI)—A USGS CEGIS perspective—Generalization and data integration: Springer, in press.

The National Map and Other USGS Data

Thomas Shoberg

Publications

Varanka, D., Carter, J., Usery, E.L., and Shoberg, T., 2011, Topographic mapping data semantics through data conversion and enhancement, *in* Ashish, N., and Sheth, A.P., eds., Geospatial semantics and the semantic web—Foundations, algorithms and applications: Springer Science and Business Media, LLC, ser., Semantic Web and Beyond, v. 12.

Shoberg, T., Stoddard, P.R., and Finn, M.P., 2012. Rejuvenating pre-GPS Era geophysical surveys using *The National Map*: Journal of Surveying Engineering, v. 138, no. 2, p. 57–65.

Shoberg, T., and Stoddard, P.R., 2012, Integrating stations from the North America gravity database into a local GPS-based land gravity survey: Journal of Applied Geophysics, v. 89, p. 83.

Shoberg, T., 2012, Buttenfield, B.P., ed., Using GIS data interpolation as an aid in the design of low station density geophysical surveys: Proceedings, GDI 2010 conference, Boulder, Colorado, June 2010.

Presentations

2012

Shoberg, T., Long, S., Corns, S., and Carlo, H., 2012, Integrating *The National Map* geospatial data into extreme events supply chain networks to improve resiliency following large-scale urban disasters: Presented at the American Association of Geographers National conference, New York, New York, February 2012.

Shoberg, T., 2012, Data integration at CEGIS: Presented at the CEGIS Yearly planning meeting, Rolla, Missouri, June 2012.

Shoberg, T., and Stoddard, P.R., 2012, Finding nothing—Algorithms to search for circular features across geospatially integrated datasets: Accepted by the American Geophysical Union for presentation in their Fall 2012 conference in San Francisco, California.

2011

Data Management Sub-Group, 2011, Proposal round-robin panel: Community for Data Integration Annual Conference, Denver, Colorado.

Shoberg, T., 2011, Data integration at CEGIS: Presented at the CEGIS yearly planning meeting, June 2011, Rolla, Missouri.

2010

Shoberg, T., and Stoddard, P.R., 2010, Integrating national database stations into GPS-based land surveys: American Geophysical Union, National Conference, San Francisco, California.

Shoberg, T., Stoddard, P.R., and Finn, M.P., 2010, Rejuvenating pre-GPS era geophysical surveys with *The National Map*: Geological Society of America, National Conference, Denver, Colorado.

Shoberg, T., 2010, Data integration at CEGIS: Presented at the CEGIS Yearly planning meeting, June 2010, Denver, Colorado.

Shoberg, T., 2010, Integrating geophysical, geological and geospatial data: GDI 2010, Generalization and Data Integration Conference, Boulder, Colorado.

Lidar Extraction and Conflation

Keith Clarke

Clarke, K., and Reginald. A., 2009, Terrain feature extraction from variable resolution Digital Elevation Models: International Cartographic Conference, 24th, Santiago, Chile, November 2009.

Archer, R., and Clarke, K., 2010, Comparison of open source terrain feature extraction algorithms for variable resolution Digital Elevation Models: Presented at Special Joint Symposium of ISPRS Technical Commission IV, AutoCarto 2010, and American Society for Photogrammetry and Remote Sensing/Cartography and Geographic Information Society (ASPRS/CaGIS) Fall Specialty Conference, Orlando, Florida, November 2010.

Publications and Presentation 2007–2012
Ontology and Geospatial Semantics
Dalia Varanka

Presentations

2007

Varanka, D., 2007, Kriging and spatial interaction—A combined approach for scaling and generalizing urbanization pressure on the environment [abs.]: International Cartographic Association workshop on Geospatial Analysis and Modeling, Spatial Structure and Dynamics of Urban Environments, 2nd, Athens, Georgia, July 2007.

Varanka, D., 2007, The rise of scientific plain style cartography in English world atlases [abs.]: North American Cartographic Information Society (NACIS) 2007, St. Louis, Missouri, October 2006, p. 12–13.

Varanka, D., 2007, Effects of raster resolution changes on agricultural non-point source pollution modeling output [abs.]: Association of American Geographers Annual Meeting, April 2007.

Varanka, D., 2007, Ontological foundations of transportation data for *The National Map* (USA) [abs.]: International Cartographic Conference abstracts with programs, XXIII, Moscow, Russia, August 2007, p. 161.

2008

Varanka, D., 2008, Topographic feature inventories for national mapping ontology [abs.]: Annual Meeting of the Association of American Geographers, Boston, Massachusetts, April, 2008.

Varanka, D., 2008, Interpolating Missouri population pressure on urbanizing natural areas [abs.]: Mid-America GIS Consortium (MAGIC), Kansas City, Missouri, April 2008.

Varanka, D., 2008, Interpolating Missouri population pressure on urbanizing natural areas: Poster presented at USGS Modeling Conference, Perdido Beach, Alabama, February 2008.

Varanka, D., 2008, Krigingo metodas: populiacijos daroma spaudimo urbanizuojant gamtą matavimas ir apibendrinimas (A Kriging Approach for Scaling and Generalizing Population Pressure on Urbanizing Natural Areas) [abs.]: Mokslo ir Kūrybos Simpoziumas, XIV, (World Lithuanian Symposium on the Arts and Sciences, 14th), Lemont, Illinois, November 2008.

Varanka, D., 2008, Ontology research for *The National Map*: Spatial Ontology Community of Practice Workshop, MITRE, McLean, Virginia, October 2008.

Varanka, D., 2008, National topographic modeling, ontology-driven geographic information in the context of *The National Map*: International Workshop, 1st, on Information Semantics and its Implications for Geographical Analysis (ISGA '08) at GIScience 2008, the International Conference on Geographic Information Science, 5th, Park City, Utah, September 2008.

2009

Varanka, D., 2009, A Topographic feature taxonomy for a U.S. National topographic mapping ontology: International Cartography Conference, Santiago, Chile, November, 2009.

Varanka, D., 2009, Landscape features, technology codes, and semantics in U.S. National topographic mapping databases: The International Conference on Advanced Geographic Information Systems and Web Services (GEOWS), Cancun, Mexico, February 2009.

Varanka, D., 2009, Report on building ontology for *The National Map*: UCGIS/USGS Specialist Workshop, UCGIS Winter Assembly, Washington, D.C., February 2009.

Varanka, D., 2009, Building ontology for *The National Map*: Presentation at the Joint Mid-Continent Geographic Science Center/Center for Advanced Spatial Technologies, University of Arkansas, exploratory research meeting, Rolla, Missouri, April 2009.

2010

Varanka, D., 2010, The diffusion of U.S. Geological Survey digital geospatial data products for research and public use [abs.]: International Symposium on the History of Cartography, 3rd, University of Texas at Arlington, Arlington, Texas, October 2010.

Varanka, D.E., and Caro, H.K., 2010, Spatial relation predicates for National topographic ontologies—Cognitive and linguistic aspects of geographic space in the age of ontology and cyber-infrastructure, Las Navas del Marques, Avila Province, Spain, July 2010.

Varanka, D., and Jerris, T., 2010, Ontology Patterns for complex topographic features: AutoCarto 2010, Orlando Florida. November 2010.

Varanka, D., Bulen, A., and Carter, J.J., 2010, Triple data from *The National Map*. D.: Annual Spatial Ontology Community of Practice (SOCoP) Workshop, 3rd, Reston, Virginia, December 2010.

2011

Varanka, D., 2011, Building ontology for *The National Map*: USGS National Geospatial Program Products and Services Leads Research Meeting, January 2011.

Varanka, D.E., 2011, A topographic feature vocabulary for ontology development: GeoVoCamp, Washington, D.C., June 2011.

Varanka, D., 2011, Semantic web technology for *The National Map* [abs.]: *The National Map* Users Conference: Denver, Colorado, May 2011.

Usery, E.L., and Varanka, D., 2011, Semantics for complex features from images [abs.]: American Society for Photogrammetry and Remote Sensing 2011 Annual Conference, Milwaukee, Wisconsin, May 2011.

Varanka, D., 2011, Building ontology for *The National Map*–So Far * * *: Presented at the Community for Data Integration, Semantic Web Working Group, monthly meeting, September 2011.

Usery, E.L., and Varanka, D.E., 2011, USGS needs and advancements in semantics of geospatial data and cyber GIS: Annual Spatial Ontology Community of Practice Workshop, 4th, Reston, Virginia, December 2011.

2012

Usery, E.L., and Varanka, D., 2012, Geomorphic features on the semantic web [abs.]: Annual Meeting of the Association of American Geographers, New York, New York, April 2012.

Varanka, D.E., 2012, Semantic technology research in support of *The National Map*: USGS Core Science Systems (CSS) Senior Staff Meeting, March, 2012.

Varanka, D.E., 2012, Geospatial semantics, a basic introduction: Introduction to Geospatial Semantics and Technology Workshop, University Consortium for Geographic Information Science (UCGIS) Symposium, Washington, D.C., May 2012.

Varanka, D.E., 2012, Topographic feature type vocabularies for ontology design patterns: Institute of Electrical and Electronics Engineers (IEEE) International Geoscience and Remote Sensing Symposium (IGARSS), July 2012.

Varanka, D.E., 2012, Rethinking the meaning of data for integrated science problem solving: EarthScienceOntolog, August 2012.

Varanka, D.E., 2012, Topographic predicate vocabularies for ontology patterns: AutoCarto 2012, September, 2012.

Publications

Varanka, D.E., 2006, National trends regarding aggregate materials for urban development, with a method for the analysis of aggregates distribution, *in* Rates, trends, causes, and consequences of urban land-use change in the United States: U.S. Geological Survey Professional Paper 1726, p. 45–54.

Varanka, D.E., 2006, Interpreting map art with a perspective learned from J.M. Blaut: Cartographic Perspectives, n. 53, p. 15–23.

Varanka, D.E., 2006, Centralization and locality in the 20th century National topographic mapping program in the United States: *in* Postnikov, A., ed., Development of Ideas and methods in cartography: Moscow, Russia, Russian Academy of Sciences, p. 26–41.

Varanka, D.E., 2007, Ontological foundations of transportation data for *The National Map* (USA): Proceedings, International Cartographic Conference, XXIII, Moscow, Russia, August 2007, 13 p. (CD-ROM).

Varanka, D.E., and Shaver, D.K., 2007, Land-use change trends in the interior river lowlands ecoregion: U.S. Geological Survey Scientific Investigations Report 2007–5145, p. 12.

Varanka, D., 2008, Interpolating population pressure on urbanizing natural areas (poster): Rolla, Missouri.

Varanka, D.E., 2008, National Topographic modeling, ontology-driven geographic information in the context of *The National Map*: International Workshop on Information Semantics and its Implications for Geographical Analysis, 1st, (ISGA '08) at GIScience 2008, the International Conference on Geographic Information Science, 5th, Park City, Utah, September 2008.

Usery, E.L., Varanka, D.E., and Finn, M.P., 2009, 125 Years of topographic mapping, Part 1, 1884–1980: Esri ArcNews, v. 31, no. 3, p. 1.

Usery, E.L., Varanka, D.E., and Finn, M., 2009, USGS history, Part 2—From the dawn of digital to *The National Map*, 125 years of topographic mapping, Part 2: Esri ArcNews, vol. 31, no. 4, p. 39.

Varanka, D.E., 2009, Landscape features, technology codes, and semantics in U.S. National topographic mapping databases: The International Conference on Advanced Geographic Information Systems and Web Services (GEOWS), Cancun, Mexico, February 2009.

Usery, E.L., Varanka, D.E., and Finn, M., 2009, A 125 year history of topographic mapping and GIS in the USGS, 1884–2009: International Cartography Conference, Santiago, Chile, November 2009.

Varanka, D.E., 2009, A Topographic feature taxonomy for a U.S. National topographic mapping ontology: International Cartography Conference, Santiago, Chile, November 2009.

Varanka, D., 2009, Interpreting Missouri population pressure on urbanizing natural areas [poster], *in* Madden, M., ed., Manual of Geographic Information Systems (GIS) Supplemental DVD: Bethesda, Maryland, American Society for Photogrammetry and Remote Sensing (ASPRS).

Varanka, D.E., and Usery, E.L., 2010, Special section, Ontological issues for *The National Map*: Cartographica—The International Journal for Geographic Information and Visualization, v. 45, no. 2, p. 103–104.

Varanka, D.E., 2010, Interpolating a consumption variable for scaling and generalizing potential population pressure on urbanizing natural areas, *in* Jiang, B., and Yao, X., eds., Geospatial analysis and modeling of urban structure and dynamics: New York, New York, Springer Publishing Company, p. 293–310.

Varanka, D.E., 2010, Ontology, *in* Warf, B., ed., Encyclopedia of geography: Thousand Oaks, California, Sage Publications, Inc.

Varanka, D.E., and Jerris, T., 2010, Ontology design patterns for complex topographic features: AutoCarto 2010, Orlando, Florida, November 2010.

Varanka, D.E., 2011, Ontology design patterns for complex topographic feature types: Cartography and Geographic Information Science, v. 38, no. 2, p. 126–136.

Varanka, D.E., 2011, Advances toward expanding gazetteer semantics: International Cartography Conference, Paris, France.

Caro, H.K., and Varanka, D.E., 2011, Analysis of spatial relation predicates in U.S. Geological Survey feature definitions: U.S. Geological Survey Open-File Report 2011–1235, 37 p.

Bulen, A.N., Carter, J.J., and Varanka, D.E., 2011, A program for the conversion of *The National Map* data from proprietary format to Resource Description Framework (RDF): U.S. Geological Survey Open-File Report 2011–1142, 9 p.

Varanka, D., 2011, *The National Map* geospatial semantic linked data: U.S. Geological Survey Information Product. (poster).

Varanka, D.E., Carter, J.J., Shoberg, T., and Usery, E.L., 2011, Topographic mapping data semantics through data conversion and enhancement, *in* Ashish, N., and Sheth, A.P., eds., Geospatial semantics and the semantic web—Foundations, algorithms, and applications: Springer, ser. Semantic Web and Beyond Computing for Human Experience, v. 12, p. 145–162.

Varanka, D.E., Deering, C. and Caro, H., 2012, The use of U.S. Geological Survey digital geospatial data products for science research, *in* Elri Liebenberg and Imre Demhardt, eds., History of Cartography. [Lecture notes *in* Geoinformation and Cartography: Springer, Berlin, v. 6, part 3, p. 129–141.]

Usery, E.L., and Varanka, D.E., 2012, Design and development of linked data for *The National Map*: The Semantic Web Journal.

Varanka, D.E., 2012, Introduction to geospatial semantics and technology workshop handbook: U.S. Geological Survey Open-File Report 2012–1109, 107 p.

Varanka, D.E., and Usery, E.L., 2012, Topographic feature type vocabularies for ontology design patterns: Institute of Electrical and Electronics Engineers (IEEE) International Geoscience and Remote Sensing Symposium (IGARSS), July 2012.

Varanka, D., and Caro, H., 2013, Spatial relation predicates for topographic data triples, *in* Raubal, M., Andrew, A.U., and Mark, D.M., eds., Cognitive and linguistic aspects of geographical space: Springer, 21 p.

Publications and Presentation 2007–2012
User Centered Design
(VGI, Crowdsourcing and Social Media)

Barbara Poore

Poore, B., and Wolf, E., 2012, Metadata squared—Enhancing its usability for volunteered geographic information and the GeoWeb, D.Z., Sui, Elwood, S., and Goodchild, M.F., eds. *in* Volunteered geographic information, public participation, and crowdsourced production of geographic knowledge: Berlin, Springer.

Liu, S.B., Poore, B., and Earle, P., 2012, Geospatial crowdsourcing—A typology of crowdsourcing for the emergency management domain: Cartography and Geographic Information Science, special issue on Mapping Cyberspace and Social Media.

Presentations

2012

Wolf, E., 2012, I fight authority, authority always wins: Annual Meeting of the Association of American Geographers, New York, New York; WhereCampTB, Saint Petersburg, Florida, February; and AutoCarto 2013, Columbus, Ohio, September 2012.

Poore, B., Wolf, E., and Matthews, G., 2012, The integration of crowdsourced data into spatial data infrastructures: issues and future prospects: Presented by Poore at the Global Spatial Data Infrastructure (GSDI'13), Quebec City, Canada, May 2012.

Poore, B., Wolf, E., and Liu, S., 2012, Citizen science and social media for *The National Map*: Presented by Poore and Liu at the CEGIS annual meeting, Rolla, Missouri, June 2012.

Poore, B., and Wolf, E., 2012, What does the USGS need to consider when designing policy for citizen science projects?: Presented by Wolf at the USGS Citizen Science Workshop, Denver, Colorado, September 2012.

Poore, B., Wolf, E., and Matthews, G., 2012, Engaging citizens to update *The National Map* at the USGS: Presented by Wolf at AutoCarto Columbus, Ohio, September 2012.

VGI and Social Media for The National Map

Refereed Publications

Liu, S.B., Poore, B., and Earle, P., 2012, Geospatial crowdsourcing—A typology of crowdsourcing for the emergency management domain: Cartography and Geographic Information Science, special issue on Mapping Cyberspace and Social Media.

Poore, B., and Wolf, E., 2012, Metadata squared—Enhancing its usability for volunteered geographic information and the GeoWeb, D.Z., Sui, Elwood, S., and Goodchild, M.F., eds., *in* Volunteered geographic information, public participation, and crowdsourced production of geographic knowledge: Springer, Berlin.

Poore, B., 2011, Users as essential contributors to spatial cyberinfrastructures: Proceedings, National Academy of Sciences, v. 108, no. 4, p. 5504–5509.

Poore, B., 2010, Wall-e and the many, many maps—Toward user-centred ontologies for *The National Map*: Cartographica, v. 45, no. 2, p. 113–20.

Wilson, M., and Poore, B., 2009, Repositioning critical GIS: Cartographica, v. 44, no. 1, p. 6–7. Edited special issue.

Reports

Poore, B., Wolf, E., Korris, E., Walter, J., and Matthews, G., 2012, Structures data collection for *The National Map* using volunteered geographic information: U.S. Geological Survey, Open-File Report 2012–1209, p. 34.

Bristol, R., Euliss, N., Jr., Booth, N., Burkardt, N., Diffendorfer, J., Gesch, D., McCallum, B., Miller, D., Morman, S., Poore, B., Signell, R., and Viger, R., 2012, Science strategy for core science systems in the U.S. Geological Survey 2013–2023: U.S. Geological Survey, Open-File Report: 2012–1093, p. 29.

Wolf, E.G., Matthews, K., McNinch, Kevin, and Poore, B., 2011, Openstreetmap collaborative prototype, Phase 1: U.S. Geological Survey Open-File Report: 2011–1136, p. 23.

Poore, B., 2011, U.S. Geological Survey and Open GISconsortium, Jankowski, P., ed., *in* Encyclopedia of Geography: Thousand Oaks, California, Sage Publications, p. 77.

Sugarbaker, Larry, Coray, K., and Poore, B., 2009, *The National Map* Customer Requirements—Findings from interviews and surveys: U.S. Geological Survey Open-File Report 2009–1222, p. 34.

Workshops

Poore, B., Co-organized USGS Citizen Science Workshop: Community for Data Integration: Denver, Colorado, September 2012.

Poore, B., Co-organized workshop law and the Geoweb: Microsoft Research and the Association of American Geographers, [with Puneet Kishor of Creative Commons] Seattle, Washington, April 2011.

Poore, B., Co-organized workshop Volunteered geographic information: U.S. Geological Survey, Herndon, Virginia [with Kari Kraun and Morgan Bearden], January 2010.

Invited talks

Poore, B., 2011, Always in beta, Invited talk, mapping democracy—technology, social change, and Web 2.0 Conference, University of Colorado—Boulder, September 2011.

Poore, B., 2010, Slow maps: Microsoft Research Forum, New York University, January 2012.

Poore, B., 2010, CyberGIS—Learning from users—CyberGIS workshop: National Science Foundation and the University Consortium for Geographical Information Science, Washington, D.C., February 2010.

Poore, B., 2010, The metadata crisis—Can geographic information be made more usable?: Workshop on Geographic Data Usability, 2nd, sponsored by the Ordnance Survey, University of Nottingham and University College—London, London, England, 2010.

Poore, B. Mapping the unmappable—Is it possible, ethical, or even desirable to incorporate volunteered geographic information into scientific projects?: Workshop on the Role of Volunteered Geographic Information in Science, sponsored by Oak Ridge National Laboratory and University of California, Santa Barbara, Zurich, Switzerland, September 2010.

Technical Presentations

Wolf, E., 2012, I fight authority, authority always wins: Annual Meeting of the Association of American Geographers, New York, New York; WhereCampTB, Saint Petersburg, Florida, February; and AutoCarto 2013, Columbus, Ohio, September 2012.

Poore, B., Wolf, E., and Matthews, E.G., 2012, The integration of crowdsourced data into spatial data infrastructures—Issues and future prospects: Presented by Poore at the Global Spatial Data Infrastructure (GSDI'13), Quebec City, Canada, May 2012.

Poore, B., and Liu, S., 2012, Citizen science and social media for *The National Map*: CEGIS annual meeting, Rolla, Missouri, June 2012.

Poore, B., 2012, What does the USGS need to consider when designing policy for citizen science projects?: Presented by Wolf at the USGS Citizen Science Workshop, Denver Colorado, September 2012.

Poore, B., and Matthews, G., 2012, Engaging citizens to update *The National Map* at the USGS: Presented by Wolf at AutoCarto 2012, Columbus, Ohio, September 2012.

Poore, B., 2011, User-centered design for *The National Map*: CEGIS Annual Meeting, Rolla, Missouri.

Wolf, E., 2011, GeoData workshop, Broomfield, Colorado, March 2011.

Poore, B., 2011, Volunteered geographic information at the U.S. Geological Survey. Where 2.0 conference Santa Clara, California, O'Reilly Media, 2011.

Poore, B., 2011, The OpenStreetMap collaborative prototype: 2011 NC GIS Conference, Raleigh, North Carolina, 2011.

Poore, B., 2011, OpenStreetMap and the U.S. Geological Survey: WhereCampDC 2011, Washington, D.C., 2011.

Poore, B., 2010, OpenStreetMap and the U.S. Geological Survey: WhereCamp5280 2010, Denver, Colorado, 2010.

Poore, B., 2009, Ethics and GIS—Philosophy and GIS, user issues in GIS for cloud computing: Panel Sessions at the Annual Meeting of the Association of American Geographers, Las Vegas, Nevada 2009.

Poore, B., 2010, What a long strange trip it's been—Mapping and virtual community from The Grateful Dead to OpenStreet-Map: International Symposium on the History of Cartography, 3rd, Arlington, Texas, October 2009.

Poore, B., 2009, Volunteered geographic information: discussant at a paper session and respondent to a plenary address by Dr. Michael Goodchild, University of California, Santa Barbara at the Annual Meeting of the Association of American Geographers, Las Vegas, Nevada, March 2009.

Poore, B., 2009, Wall-e and the many, many, maps—Ontologies for distributed collaboration: UCGIS/USGS Ontology for *The National Map* Specialists Meeting, Washington, D.C., February 2009.

Poore, B., and Finn, M., 2008, Who will use cyberinfrastructure and how? Cyberinfrastructure for GIScience Workshop: National Science Foundation and GIScience 2008, Park City, Utah, 2008.

Poore, B., 2008, Mapping without maps: What about the users of GIS?: GIScience 2008, Park City, Utah, September 2008.

Poore, B., 2008, Push-pin geography—Implications for the design of user-centered interfaces for internet mapping: Association of American Geographers Annual Meeting, Boston, Massachusetts, 2008.

Poore, B., and Finn, M., 2008, User-C=centered cesign for spatial data infrastructures—Implications of new Internet technologies: Auto-Carto 2008, Shepherdstown, West Virginia, September 2008.

Poore, B., and Finn, M., 2009, User-centered design for *The National Map*, *in* Lavoie, D.L., Rosen, B.H., Sumner, D.M, Haag, K.H., Tihansky, A.B., Boynton, A.B., and Koenig, R.R.,eds., USGS Gulf Coast Science Conference and Florida Integrated Science Center (FISC) Meeting, Proceedings with Abstracts, Orlando, Florida, October 2008: U.S. Geological Survey Open-File Report 2009–1329, p. 137. (poster presentation).

Software Development

Wolf, E., Submitted OpenStreetMap Collaborative Project Software to Map Mashup Contest at the U.S. Geological Survey *The National Map*.

Publications and Presentation 2007–2012

**Multi-resolution Raster
(High Performance Computing)**

Michael P. Finn

2012

Behzad, Babak, Yan Liu, Eric Shook, Michael P. Finn, David M. Mattli, and Shaowen Wang, 2012, A Performance profiling strategy for high-performance map re-projection of coarse-scale spatial raster data [abs.]: Auto-Carto 2012, A Cartography and Geographic Information Society Research Symposium, Columbus, Ohio, 2012.

Finn, Michael P., Daniel R. Steinwand, Jason R. Trent, Robert A. Buehler, David Mattli, and Kristina H. Yamamoto, 2012, A program for handling map projections of small scale geospatial raster data: Cartographic Perspectives, no.71, p. 53–67.

Finn, Michael P., Gary W. Krizanich, Kevin R. Evans, Melissa R. Cox, and Kristina H. Yamamoto, 2012, Visualizing impact structures using high-resolution LiDAR derived DEMs—A case study of two structures in Missouri: Surveying and Land Information Science, v. 72, no. 2, pp. 87–97.

Finn, Michael P., Yan Liu, David M. Mattli, Qingfeng (Gene) Guan, Kristina H. Yamamoto, Eric Shook and Babak Behzad, 2012, pRasterBlaster—High-Performance small-scale raster map projection transformation using the extreme science and engineering discovery environment [abs.]: International Society for Photogrammetry and Remote Sensing Congress, XXII, Melbourne, Australia, 2012.

Finn, Michael P., Yan Liu, David M. Mattli, Babak Behzad, Kristina H. Yamamoto, Anand Padmanabhan, and Michael Stramel, 2012, Raster map projection transformation using a virtual system to interactively share computing resources: International Conference on Space, Time, and CyberGIS (CyberGIS'12), 1st, Urbana-Champaign, Illinois, 2012. (presentation).

Mattli, David, Michael P. Finn, and Michael Stramel, 2012, pRasterBlaseter—Fast, accurate raster reprojection: International Conference on Space, Time, and CyberGIS (CyberGIS'12), 1st, Urbana-Champaign, Illinois, 2012. (poster).

Yamamoto, Kristina H., and Michael P. Finn, 2012, Approximating tasseled-cap values to evaluate brightness, greenness, and wetness for the advanced land imager (ALI): U.S. Geological Survey Scientific Investigation Report 2012–5057, 9 p.

Shoberg, Tom, Paul Stoddard and Michael P. Finn, 2012, Rejuvenating pre-GPS era geophysical surveys using the National Map: Journal of Surveying Engineering, v. 138, no. 2, May 1. (Available at *ISSN 0733-9453/2012/2-0-0/.*)

Finn, Michael P., and David M. Mattli, 2012, User's guide for the mapIMG 3—Map image reprojection software package: U.S. Geological Survey Open-File Report 2011–1306, 12 p.

Finn, Michael P., Mark (David) Lewis, David D. Bosch, Mario Giraldo, Kristina Yamamoto, Dana G. Sullivan, Russell Kincaid, Ronaldo Luna, Gopala Krishna Allam, Craig Kvien, and Michael S. Williams, 2011, Remote sensing of soil moisture using airborne hyperspectral data: GIScience and Remote Sensing v. 48, no. 4, p. 522–540.

Wood, Elisa C., and Michael P. Finn, 2011, Digitization of the bibliography of map projections: Conference of the International Cartographic Association, 25th, Paris, France, 2012. (poster).

2010

Shoberg, Tom, Paul Stoddard, and Michael P. Finn, 2010, Rejuvenating pre-GPS era geophysical surveys using *The National Map*: 2010 Geological Society of America Annual Meeting, Denver, Colorado, 2010. (poster).

Finn, Michael P., and Holly K. Caro, 2010, The CEGIS on-line bibliography—A resource for the working GIScientist [abs.]: Association of American Geographers Annual Meeting, Washington, D.C., 2010.

Usery, E. Lynn, Jinmu Choi, and Michael P. Finn, 2010, Modeling sea level rise and surge in low-lying urban areas using spatial data, geographic information systems, and animation methods, *in* Pamela S. Showalter and Yongmei Lu, eds., Geospatial techniques in urban hazard and disaster analysis: Springer-Verlag., chap. 2.

2009

Finn, Michael P., and Barbara S. Poore, 2009, Endeavors to serve digital geospatial data as a commonly offered cache of topographic information [abs.]: Joint International Workshop of International Society for Photogrammetry and Remote Sensing, Technical Commission IV, Working Group IV/1 and Technical Commission, VIII, Working Group VIII on Geospatial Data CyberInfrastructure and Real-time Services with special emphasis on Disaster Management, Hyderabad, India, 2009.

Giraldo, Mario A., David Bosch, Marguerite Madden, Lynn Usery, and Michael P. Finn, 2009, Ground and surface temperature variability for remote sensing of soil moisture in a heterogeneous landscape: Journal of Hydrology, v. 368, issues 1–4, p. 214–223.

Guan, Qingfeng, Michael P. Finn, E. Lynn Usery, and David M. Mattli, 2009, Rapid raster projection transformation and web service using high-performance computing technology [abs.]: Association of American Geographers Annual Meeting, Las Vegas, Nevada, 2009.

Krizanich, Gary W., and Michael P. Finn, 2009, Table Rock Lake water quality assessment using landsat thematic mapper satellite data: U.S. Geological Survey Scientific Investigation Report 2009–5162, p. 9.

Stanislawski, Lawrence V., Barbara P. Buttenfield, Michael P. Finn, and Keven Roth, 2009, Stratified database pruning to support local density variations in automated generalization of the United States National Hydrography Dataset: Proceedings, International Cartographic Conference, Santiago, Chile, 2009.

Usery, E. Lynn, David D. Bosch, Michael P. Finn, Tasha Wells, Stuart Pocknee, and Craig Kvien, 2009, GIS in precision agriculture and watershed management, *in* Madden, M., ed., Manual of GIS: Bethesda, Maryland, American Society of Photogrammetry and Remote Sensing, chap. 2.

Usery, E. Lynn, Michael P. Finn, and Clifford J. Mugnier, 2009, Coordinate systems and map projections, *in* Madden, M., ed., Manual of GIS: Bethesda, Maryland, American Society of Photogrammetry and Remote Sensing, chap. 8.

Usery, E. Lynn, Michael P. Finn, and Michael Starbuck, 2009, Data layer integration for *The National Map* of the United States: Cartographic Perspectives, no. 62, Winter 2009, p. 28–41.

Usery, E. Lynn, Dalia Varanka, and Michael P. Finn, 2009, A 125 year history of topographic mapping and GIS in the U.S. Geological Survey 1884–2009, Part 1—1884–1980: Esri ArcNews, Fall 2009, v. 31, no. 3, p. 1.

Usery, E. Lynn, Dalia Varanka, and Michael P. Finn, 2009, A 125 Year history of topographic mapping and GIS in the U.S. Geological Survey 1884–2009, Part 2—1980–2009: Esri ArcNews, Winter 2009/2010, v. 31, no. 4, p. 39.

Usery, E. Lynn, Dalia Varanka, and Michael P. Finn, 2009, A 125 Year history of topographic mapping and GIS in the USGS: 1884–2009: Proceedings, International Cartographic Conference, Santiago, Chile, 2009.

Wolf, Eric B., Kevin Howe, Michael P. Finn, and Barbara S. Poore, 2009, Functional analysis for *The National Map* server-side computing [abs.]: Association of American Geographers Annual Meeting, Las Vegas, Nevada, 2009.

Wu, Shou-Sheng, E. Lynn Usery, Michael P. Finn, and David D. Bosch, 2009, Effects of sampling interval on spatial patterns and statistics of watershed nitrogen concentration: GIScience and Remote Sensing, v. 46, no. 2, p. 1–15.

2008

Finn, Michael P., and Barbara S. Poore, 2008, Towards a User-Centered Design (UCD) for *The National Map* of the U.S. Geological Survey [abs.]: Congress of the International Society for Photogrammetry and Remote Sensing, XXI, Beijing, China, 2008.

Finn, Michael P., Barbara S. Poore, and Mark R. Feller, 2008, Towards a more consistent framework for disseminated spatial computing for *The National Map* [abs.]: Association of American Geographers Annual Meeting, Boston, Massachusettes, 2008.

Finn, Michael P., and E. Lynn Usery, 2008, Implementing a research agenda to address challenging geographic information science issues [abs.]: U.S. Geological Survey Geographic Information Systems Workshop, Denver, Colorado, 2008.

Poore, Barbara S., and Michael P. Finn, 2008, User-centered design for spatial data infrastructures: implications of new internet technologies: Proceedings: Auto-Carto 2008, A Cartography and Geographic Information Society Research Symposium, Shepherdstown, West Virginia, 2008.

Usery, E. Lynn, Jinmu Choi, and Michael P. Finn, 2008, Elements of a global model—An example of sea level rise and human populations at risk: Proceedings, U.S. Geological Survey Modeling Conference, Perdido Beach, Alabama, 2008.

Wu, Shou-Sheng, E. Lynn Usery, Michael P. Finn, and David D. Bosch, 2008, An assessment of the effects of cell sizes on AGNPS Modeling of watershed runoff: Cartography and Geographic Information Science, v. 35, no. 4, p. 265–278.

2007

Finn, Michael P., Gary W. Krizanich, Kevin R. Evans, and E. Lynn Usery, 2007, Contemporary high-resolution LiDAR derived DEMs could inspire developments in the study of impact structures: Proceedings, Association of American Geographers/ Great Plains—Rocky Mountain Section Annual Meeting, Denver, Colorado, 2007.

Finn, Michael P., Gary W. Krizanich, and E. Lynn Usery, 2007, Contemporary high-resolution LiDAR derived DEMs could inspire developments in the study of impact structures: Proceedings, International Union of Geodesy and Geophysics, XXIV, General Assembly, Perugia, Italy, p. 408–409.

Lewis, David and Michael P Finn, 2007, Soil moisture estimation using hyperspectral SWIR imagery: The American Geophysical Union Annual Meeting, San Francisco, California, 2007. (poster).

Ruhl, Shelia, E. Lynn Usery, and Michael P. Finn, 2007, EL86D Wasteway watershed land cover generation: U.S. Geological Survey Open-File Report 2007–1143, 28 p.

Stanislawski, Larry, Michael P. Finn, Mark Barnes, and E. Lynn Usery, 2007, Assessment of a rapid approach for estimating catchment areas for surface drainage lines: Proceedings, American Congress on Surveying and Mapping 2007 Annual Conference, St. Louis, Missouri, 2007.

Stanislawski, Larry, Michael P. Finn, and E. Lynn Usery, 2007, Development of a blunder detection approach for automated point matching during vector to image data integration: Proceedings, American Society for Photogrammetry and Remote Sensing 2007 Annual Conference, Tampa, Florida.

Usery, E. Lynn, Jinmu Choi, and Michael P. Finn, 2007, Modeling sea-level rise effects on population using global elevation and land-cover data: Proceeedings, Association of American Geographers, Annual Conference, San Francisco, California, 2007.

Usery, E. Lynn and Michael P. Finn, 2007, Cartographic Research at the U.S. Geological Survey Center of Excellence for Geo-Spatial Information science: Proceedings, International Cartographic Conference, XXIII, Moscow, Russia.

Wu, Shou-Sheng, E. Lynn Usery, and Michael P. Finn, 2007, Effects of sampling interval on spatial analysis of watershed nitrogen loading: Proceedings, International Conference on Environmental Science and Technology, 3rd, Houston, Texas, 2007.

2006

Finn, Michael P., David D. Bosch, E. Lynn Usery, and Austin D. Hartman, 2006, Problems associated with comparing in situ Water quality measurements to pollution model output for geographic analyses [abs.]: Association of American Geographer, Annual Conference, Chicago, Illinois, 2006.

Finn, Michael P., Jason R. Trent, and Robert A. Buehler, 2006, User's guide for the map image re-projection software package, version 2.1: U.S. Geological Survey Open-File Report 2006–1016, p. 19.

Finn, Michael P., E. Lynn Usery, Douglas J. Scheidt, Gregory M. Jaromack, and Timothy D. Krupinski, 2006, An interface between the Agricultural Non-Point Source (AGNPS) pollution model and the ERDAS Imagine Geographic Information System (GIS): Geographic Information Sciences, June 2006, v. 12, no. 1, p. 9–19.

Finn, Michael P., Michael S. Williams, and E. Lynn Usery, 2006, An Implementation of the jenks-caspall algorithm for optimal classification of data for geographic visualization: American Society for Photogrammetry and Remote Sensing Annual Conference, Reno, Nevada, 2006. (poster).

Stanislawski, Larry, Michael P. Finn, Michael Starbuck, E. Lynn Usery, and Patrick Turley, 2006, Estimation of accumulated upstream drainage values in braided streams using augmented directed graphs: Proceedings, Auto-Carto 2006, A Cartography and Geographic Information Society Research Symposium, Vancouver, Washington, 2006.

Williams, Michael S., Michael P. Finn, and Robert A. Buehler, 2006, An open source, object-oriented General Cartographic Transformation Program (GCTP) [abs.]: International Society for Photogrammetry and Remote Sensing Commission, IV, Symposium on Geospatial Databases for Sustainable Development, Goa, India, 2006.

CEGIS Publications and Presentations 2006–2012

E. Lynn Usery

Publications

Usery, E.L., 2005, Geography for a changing world: Bulletin of the American Congress on Surveying and Mapping, no. 217, p. 23–24.

Arpinar, I.B., Sheth, A., Ramakrishnan, C., Usery, E.L., Azami, M., and Kwan, M., 2006, Geospatial Ontology development and semantic analytics: Transactions in GIS, v. 10, no. 4, p. 551–576.

Ling, Y., Ehlers, M., Usery, E.L., and Madden, M., 2006, Enhanced IHS transform methods for fusing commercial high resolution satellite images: ISPRS Journal of Photogrammetry and Remote Sensing, v. 61, no. 6, p. 381–392.

Finn, M.P., Usery, E.L., Scheidt, D.J., Jaromack, G.M., and Krupinski, T.D., 2006, An Interface between the Agricultural Non-Point Source (AGNPS) pollution model and the ERDAS imagine geographic information system: Geographic Information Sciences, v. 12, no. 1, p. 10–20.

Knoblock, C.A., Chen, C.C., and Usery, E.L., 2006, Automatic alignment of vector data and orthoimagery for *The National Map*: Digital Government Conference, San Diego, California, 2006.

Stanislawski, L., Finn, M.P., Starbuck, M., Usery, E.L., and Turley, P., 2006, Estimation of accumulated upstream drainage values in braided streams using augmented directed graphs: Proceedings, Auto Carto 2006, Vancouver, Washington, 2006.

Ruhl, S., Usery, E.L., and Finn, M.P., 2006, EL68D wasteway land cover generation: U.S. Geological Survey Open-File Report 2007–1143, p. 28.

Stanislawski, L., Finn, M.P., Usery, E.L., and Robinette, P.L., 2007, Development of a blunder detection approach for automated point matching during vector to image data integration: Proceedings, American Society for Photogrammetry and Remote Sensing Annual Conference, Tampa, Florida, 2007.

Stanislawski, L., Finn, M.P., Barnes, M., and Usery, E.L., 2007, Assessment of a rapid approach for estimating catchment areas for surface drainage lines: Proceedings, Amercian Congress on Surveying and Mapping Annual Conference, St. Louis, Missouri, 2007.

Usery, E.L., and Finn, M.P., 2007, Cartographic research at the U.S. Geological Survey Center of Excellence for Geospatial Information Science: Proceedings, International Cartographic Conference, Moscow, Russia, 2007.

Wei, M., Zhao, T., Varanka, D., and Usery, E.L, 2008, A conceptual design towards semantic geospatial access: GIScience 2008, Park City, Utah, 2008. (poster).

Giraldo, M.A., Bosch, D., Madden, M., Usery, E.L., and Kvien, C., 2008, Landscape complexity and soil moisture variation in South Georgia, USA, for remote sensing applications: Journal of Hydrology, v. 357, p. 405–420.

Wu, S., Qiu, X., Usery, E.L., and Wang, L., 2008, Using geometrical, textural, and contextual information of land parcels for classification of detailed urban land use: Annals of the Association of American Geographers, v. 99, no. 1, p. 76–98.

Ling, Y, Usery, E.L., Ehlers, M., and Madden, M., 2008, Effects of spatial resolution in image fusion: International Journal of Remote Sensing, v. 29, no. 7, p. 2157–2167.

Choi, J., Seong, J.C., Kim, B., and Usery, E.L., 2008, Innovations in individual feature history management—The significance of feature-based temporal model: Geoinformatica, v. 12, p. 1–20.

Giraldo, M.A., Bosch, D., Madden, M., Usery, E.L., and Kvien, C., 2008, Landscape complexity and soil moisture variation in South Georgia, USA, for remote sensing applications: Journal of Hydrology, v. 357, p. 405–420.

Brewer, C.A., Buttenfield, B.P., and Usery, E.L., 2009, Evaluating generalizations of hydrography in differing terrains for *The National Map* of The United States: Proceedings, International Cartographic Conference, Santiago, Chile, 2009.

Usery, E.L., Varanka, D., and Finn, M.P., 2009, Mapping developments and GIS in the USGS, 1884–2009: Proceedings, International Cartographic Conference, Santiago, Chile, 2009.

Usery, E.L., Finn, M.P., and Mugnier, C., 2009, Coordinate systems and map projections: Manual of Geographic Information Systems, American Society for Photogrammetry and Remote Sensing, Bethesda, Maryland, p. 87–112.

Usery, E.L., Bosch, D.D., Finn, M.P., Wells, T., Pocknee, S., and Kvien, C., 2009, GIS in Precision agriculture and watershed management: Manual of Geographic Information Systems: American Society for Photogrammetry and Remote Sensing, Bethesda, Maryland, p. 1169–1198.

Le, Y., and Usery, E.L., 2009, Adding time to GIS: Manual of Geographic Information Systems, American Society for Photogrammetry and Remote Sensing, Bethesda, Maryland, p. 311–332.

Usery, E.L., Choi, J., and Finn, M.P., 2009, Modeling Sea-level rise and surge in low-lying urban areas using spatial data, geographic information systems, and animation methods, *in* Showalter, P., and Lu, Y., (eds.), Geospatial techniques in urban hazard and disaster analysis: Springer, Dordrecht, p. 11–20.

Fleming, S., Jordan, T., Madden, M., Usery, E.L., and Welch, R., 2009, GIS applications for military operations in coastal zones: ISPRS Journal of Photogrammetry and Remote Sensing, v. 64, p. 213–222.

Wu, S., Usery, E.L., Finn, M.P., and Bosch, D., 2009, An assessment of the effects of cell size on AGNPS modeling of watershed runoff: Cartography and Geographic Information Science, v. 35, no. 4, p. 265–278.

Usery, E.L., Finn, M.P., and Starbuck, M., 2009, Data layer integration for *The National Map* of the United States: Cartographic Perspectives, v. 62, p. 28–41.

Giraldo, M.A., Bosch, D., Madden, M., Usery, E.L., and Finn, M., 2009, Ground and surface temperature variability for remote sensing of soil moisture in a heterogeneous landscape: Journal of Hydrology, v. 368, p 214–223.

Wu, S., Usery, E.L., Finn, M.P., and Bosch, D., 2009, Effects of sampling interval on spatial patterns and statistics of watershed nitrogen concentration: GIScience and Remote Sensing, v. 46, no. 2, p.172–186.

Choi, J. and Usery, E.L., 2009, A Prototype feature system for feature retrieval using relationships: Cartography and Geographic Information Science, v. 36, no. 4, p. 331–345.

Finn, M., Usery, E.L., and Reed, M., 2009, Approximating tasseled-cap values for the advanced land imager (ALI): American Society of Photogrammetry and Remote Sensing (ASPRS) Manual of Geographic Information Systems. (CD-ROM publication).

Usery, E.L., Choi, J., Finn, M., 2009, Simulating Sea Level rise and surges with geographic information datasets and animation methods: American Society of Photogrammetry and Remote Sensing (ASPRS) Manual of Geographic Information Systems. (CD-ROM publication).

Varanka, D., and Usery, E.L., 2010, Special Section: Ontological issues for *The National Map*: Cartographica—The International Journal for Geographic Information and Visualization, v. 45, no. 2, p. 103–104.

Usery, E.L., 2011, The digital transition in cartography—USGS data innovations, 1970s, *in* Liebenberg, E., and I., Demhardt, eds., History of cartography: Interanational Symposium of the International Cartographic Association (ICA) Commission, 2010, Berlin: Springer Verlag, p. 113–126.

Varanka, D., Carter, J., Usery, E.L., and Shoberg, T., 2011, Topographic mapping data semantics through data conversion and enhancement, *in* Ashish, N., and Sheth, A.P., eds., Geospatial semantics and the semantic web—Foundations, algorithms and applications: Springer, New York, p. 145–162.

Usery, E.L., and Varanka, D., 2012, Design and development of linked data from *The National Map*: Semantic Web Journal.

Usery, E.L., 2012, Generalization and Data Integration (GDI): A USGS CEGIS Perspective, Generalization and Data Integration: Springer, in press.

Presentations

Usery, E.L., 2012, The web mercator projection—The legacy continues into the electronic age: International Conference on Cartography and GIS, 4th, Albena, Bulgaria.

Usery, E.L., 2012, Geospatial semantic technology—A case study with USGS data: University Consortium for Geospatial Information Science/U.S. Geological Survey Workshop on Geospatial Semantics, Washington, D.C.

Usery, E.L., 2012, CyberGIS in the USGS—Perspective and vision: Association of American Geographers Annual Meeting, New York.

Usery, E.L., 2012, Geomorphic features on the semantic web: Association of American Geographers Annual Meeting, New York.

Usery, E.L., 2012, Geospatial semantics and CyberGIS: University of Illinois at Urbana-Champaign.

Usery, E.L., 2011, USGS Advancements in geospatial semantics and CyberGIS: Institute of Geographical Sciences and Natural Resources Research, Chinese Academy of Sciences, Beijing, China.

Usery, E.L., 2011, Data exchange for global science: U.S.-China Roundtable on Scientific Data Cooperation, Beijing, China,

Usery, E.L., 2011, USGS needs and advancements in CyberGIS: CyberGIS All-hands Meeting, Oak Ridge, Tennessee, 2011.

Usery, E.L., 2011, National geospatial data Assets maintained by the U.S. Geological Survey as Part of *The National Map*: International Cartographic Conference, Paris, France.

Usery, E.L., 2011, The U.S. National Committee and the International Cartographic Association: North American Cartographic Information Society, Madison, Wisconsin.

Usery, E.L., 2011, Ontology and semantics for *The National Map*: University of Nebraska, Department of geography, Lincoln, Nebraska.

Usery, E.L., 2011, Semantics for complex features and images: American Society for Photogrammetry and Remote Sensing, Milwaukee, Wisconsin.

Usery, E.L., 2011, CyberGIS research and implementation in the USGS: Association of American Geographers Annual Conference, Seattle, Washington.

Usery, E.L., 2010, USGS volunteered geographic information workshop: Herndon, Virginia.

Usery, E.L., 2010, Cyberinfrastructure components of *The National Map*: CyberGIS Workshop 2010, Washington, D.C.

Usery, E.L., 2010, Data Sharing—Critical for global science: U.S.-China Roundtable on Scientific Data Cooperation. Irvine, California.

Usery, E.L., 2010, The digital transition in Cartography—USGS data innovations, 1970s: International Symposium on the History of Cartography, 3rd, University of Texas at Arlington, Arlington, Texas.

Usery, E.L., 2009, *The National Map*, geospatial ontology, and the semantic web: International Semantic Web Conference, Terra Cognita Workshop, near Washington, D.C.

Usery, E.L., 2009, Mapping developments and GIS in the USGS, 1884—2009: International Cartographic Conference, Santiago, Chile.

Usery, E.L., 2009, 125 Years of topographic mapping, 80-panel exhibit of USGS topographic mapping history: Esri User Conference, San Diego, California.

Usery, E.L., 2009, Place still matters—Generalizing the National Hydrography Dataset by local terrain and climate: North American Cartographic Information Association, Sacramento, California.

Usery, E.L., 2009, The USGS Center of Excellence for Geospatial Information Science: Center of Excellence for Geospatial Information Science (CEGIS) Research Meeting, Rolla, Missouri.

Usery, E.L., 2009, Geospatial data integration—A review and a USGS approach: China-U.S. Roundtable on Scientific Data Cooperation, Qingdao, China.

Usery, E.L., 2009, Geospatial data integration—A review and a USGS approach: University of Missouri-Kansas City.

Usery, E.L., 2009, The USGS Center of Excellence for Geospatial Information Science—Spatio-temporal data model research: National Science Foundation Workshop on Geospatial and Geotemporal Informatics, Washington, D.C.

Usery, E.L., 2009, Modeling and animation of sea level rise and surge with geographic information system datasets: Missouri University of Science and Technology, Rolla, Missouri.

Usery, E.L., 2009, Resolution and resampling effects of raster data in global and regional models: National Research Council Board on Earth Sciences and Resources, Irvine, California.

Usery, E.L., 2008, The USGS Center of Excellence for Geospatial Information Science: Association of American Geographers, Boston, Massachusettes.

Usery, E.L., 2008, Modeling sea level rise and surge with geographic information system datasets: International Geographical Union, Tunis, Tunisia.

Usery, E.L., 2008, The USGS Center of Excellence for Geospatial Information Science: AutoCarto 2008, Shepherdstown, West Virginia.

Usery, E.L., 2009, Elements of a global model—An example of sea level rise and human populations at risk: U.S. Geological Survey Modeling Conference, 2nd, Orange Beach, Alabama.

Usery, E.L., 2007, The use of geospatial data, methods, models, processes, simulation, and animation to model global and regional events: National Research Council Board on Earth Sciences and Resources, Irvine, California.

Usery, E.L., 2007, From numbers to graphics; from graphics to animation: U.S. Geological Survey New England Science Forum, Providence, Rhode Island.

Usery, E.L., 2007, Modeling sea-level rise effects on population using global elevation and land-cover data: Association of American Geographers, San Francisco, California.

Usery, E.L., 2007, Data integration for *The National Map*: University of Missouri-Rolla.

Usery, E.L., 2007, Generalization for *The National Map*: University of North Carolina-Greensboro.

Usery, E.L., 2006, Geographic information science research in the U.S. Geological Survey: Association of American Geographers, Chicago, Illinois.

Usery, E.L., 2005, Integrating data layers to support *The National Map* of The United States: International Cartographic Conference, A Coruña, Spain.

Usery, E.L., 2005, Reprojecting raster data of global extent: Auto-Carto 2005, Las Vegas, Nevada.

Publishing support provided by:
  Rolla Publishing Service Center

For more information concerning this publication, contact:
  Director, USGS
  Center of Excellence for Geospatial Information Science (CEGIS)
  1400 Independence Road
  Rolla, MO 65401
  (573) 308–3837

Or visit the CEGIS Web site at:
  http://cegis.usgs.gov

Usery—Center of Excellence for Geospatial Information Science Research Plan 2013–18—Open-File Report 2013–1189